CREATING THE MULTI-AGE CLASSROOM

WRITTEN AND ILLUSTRATED BY

JANET CAUDILL BANKS, MA

CREATING THE MULTI-AGE CLASSROOM

By Janet Caudill Banks, MA

First Edition, August, 1993

Revised Edition, November, 1993

Revised Edition, April, 1995

Copyright © CATS Publications
(Creative Activities and Teaching Strategies)
8633 233rd Place S.W.
Edmonds, WA 98026
(425) 776-0344

ISBN 1-886753-03-2

Library of Congress Catalog Card Number: 95-68876

Also by Janet Caudill Banks   **Published by CATS Publications**

CURRICULUM BOOKS

Creative Projects for Independent Learners (Grades 3-8) ISBN 1-886753-02-4

Activities involve students with literature, comprehension skills, writing, spelling, research skills, and dictionary studies, while developing higher-level thinking skills. Projects are designed for individuals and small groups and help students to become self-directed learners.

Developing Research Skills (Grades 2-6) ISBN 1-886753-00-8

Activities center around plants and wild animals, as students learn various research techniques. Components include: outlining, locating information, note taking, mindmapping, report writing, editing, revising, proofreading, and investigating through higher-level inquiries.

Enhancing Research Skills (Intermediate and Middle School) ISBN 1-886753-01-6

Independent research activities on the Civil War. Students will learn about the war as they locate information, fill in an outline, take notes, organize material, write a rough draft, revise, edit, proofread, and complete a finished report. Also included are thematic research projects, using inquiries, which will promote higher-level thinking skills, while providing additional information for student reports.

Essential Learnings of Mathematics (Grades 3-6) ISBN 1-886753-04-0

An organizational framework for developing concepts and procedures throughout the strands of mathematics, following state and national standards. Includes rationale for math reform, student objectives and vocabulary, techniques for classroom management, explorations and investigations from real-life experiences, strategies for teaching problem solving, and suggestions for performance assessment.

Creating and Assessing Performance-Based Curriculum Projects (Grades K-8) ISBN 1-886753-19-9

A teacher's guide to project-based learning and performance assessment. Includes strategies for planning and writing thematic curriculum projects that contain authentic assessment tools for guiding and judging student performance. Projects are to be based on essential learnings standards, and need to provide for assessment of concepts, skills, learner characteristics, and learning processes students go through as they complete projects.

LANGUAGE GAMES (Grades 3-8)

Card games stressing language and dictionary skills, designed for partners or small groups and perfect for learning centers. Cards are printed on cardstock and need to be cut apart before playing.

Idiom Games   **"Define It or Fake It" and "Idiom's Delight"**

Multiple Meaning Games   **"Focus on the Meaning" and "What Could It Possibly Be?"**

Guide Word Games   **"Quick on the Draw" and "Guide Word Scramble"**

Synonym, Antonym, Homonym Games   **"Rocket Match Game" and "Synonym, Antonym Antics"**

Dictionary Research Board Games   **"What's My 'Cat'egory?" and "Guess Our Size"**

Context Clue Games   **"Consider the Context" and "Sensible Nonsense"**

GEOGRAPHY GAMES (Ages 10 to adult)

Card games using information about states and countries, which players read aloud to opponents as sets of clues. Opponents then try to determine which state or country is being described. On cardstock, these games are ready to play, in class, at home, and when traveling.

United States Geography-Geology Game   **"State Solutions" (includes all 50 states)**

World Geography Game   **"Country Clues" (includes 50 countries)**

DEDICATION

This book is dedicated to Ellen and Alan Lund of JOYFUL NOISE PUBLICATIONS for all of their help and encouragement in getting me started on my publishing and consulting career.

Acknowledgements to:

Joe Rice, Principal, and Ellen Lund, Lois Konecny, Jane Hodges, Jan Hamilton, Bonnie Vaughan, Ann Gillis, and Karen Nilson, my co-partners in the Multi-age Program, for their hard work and insight into how this concept should be successfully implemented.

Robert Anthony, from the University of British Columbia, for his permission to include the section on portfolio assessment with learner characteristics, as adapted from his workshop presentations in Edmonds, WA, 1992-93.

FOREWORD

This book has been written for those of you who have asked for more information on how to manage a multi-age classroom. It outlines the ideal classroom when all of the components are put in place. As a member of the team that initiated the Multi-age Elementary School Program in Edmonds, Washington, I started the first intermediate class, while two other teachers, Ellen Lund and Lois Konecny, started the primary class, under the direction of Principal Joe Rice. Our successful program continued to grow, and now includes 4-year-olds in Early Childhood Centers and a Multi-age Middle School.

I remained with the program for seven years as we watched it grow from 3 classrooms to a school of our own. My public school teaching career consisted of 33 years, including those seven years of experience with multi-age classrooms of 9-12 year-olds, as well as ten years working with split classes before we started this program. Now retired, I am working as a consultant and author, creating educational games, writing books, and teaching workshops to train teachers in multi-age education.

This book is based on my research, and experiences creating and managing my own multi-age classrooms, an extremely rewarding time in my teaching career. The students were very happy and motivated because they felt successful in school. Parents were very pleased at what they saw going on in our classrooms, and many of them became my close friends. Our principal was most insightful and guided us well. My team partners were all very caring and dedicated teachers. Acknowledgement is given to them for some of the ideas that are included in this book, as many of our projects were planned cooperatively.

I feel certain these ideas will be helpful to you and hope many children will have the opportunity to experience these rewarding activities and this effective method of instruction.

Janet C. Banks

TABLE OF CONTENTS

Student Record Forms (continued)

CREATING THE MULTI-AGE CLASSROOM

OUR VISION:

To enable each learner to develop according to his/her individual potential and to acquire the attitudes, knowledge, and skills needed for successful lifelong experiences.

OUR GOAL:

To develop lifelong learners, students who will be able to think for themselves, make wise decisions, be responsible and dependable, self-directed, and able to do research and manage their time effectively.

OUR BELIEF:

All children learn at different rates and should be able to grow in all areas with continuous progress and no fear of failure. All children can and should be successful.

OUR RESPONSIBILITY:

To create an atmosphere that is warm and caring, cooperative, motivating, active, successful, full of hands-on experiences, fair and consistent, therefore promoting success for each individual according to his/her own potential.

THE ADVANTAGES OF
MULTI-AGE CLASSROOMS

"All children can learn,
but this learning takes
place at different rates."

Each child should be given the best educational background that is possible. All children can learn, but this learning takes place at different rates, not predetermined by age or an arbitrary standard such as grade level. Each child should be given the opportunity to make continuous progress, without fear of failure.

If students are placed in multi-age centers, they will also have the advantage of being exposed to material above their usual grade level. They will have more help due to being placed with some peers who already understand material they are trying to master. Students take on the responsibility of helping others learn as well as learning from others.

Students will also have more control over their own learning and will be given more choices, therefore learning to be good decision makers. As the teacher's role changes to guiding learning rather than dispensing facts, children will exhibit greater independence and responsibility.

Therefore, students in this atmosphere will feel more safe and successful. They will be motivated to learn, more independent, able to make choices and decisions for themselves, more confident in solving problems, and more responsible for their own learning.

With a world that is changing so fast, facts alone will not do. Students will need to become lifelong learners. This is why multi-age classes are becoming the way of the future.

THE PRINCIPLES OF MULTI-AGE INSTRUCTION

1. The classroom needs to be an exciting place.

2. Each student needs to be valued at whatever level he/she might presently be.

3. Helping students to have positive self-concepts is of great importance, as students who feel good about themselves tend to be more successful.

4. Students should be allowed to make mistakes without fear of criticism, being able to learn from mistakes rather than feeling failure.

5. Promotions and retentions need to be used sparingly, however, there are times when it is developmentally appropriate to retain children on a certain level for a longer period of time, or promote them to a higher level.

6. Students need to develop empathy for others, and accept responsibility to help others as needed.

7. Children need time to experience working cooperatively and collaboratively with others.

8. As children interact with others, they will be learning lifelong interpersonal skills.

9. Children need to learn to share ideas and to accept the ideas of others.

10. Experiences must be provided that are active in nature, where students can learn through manipulation of objects and materials. Mobility should be an integral part of instruction.

11. Children should be given the time to create and to express themselves creatively, sharing thoughts and feelings with one another.

12. A great deal of time needs to be devoted to hands-on experiences, either in groups, or as individuals.

13. Communicating with others should fill the major part of a day, both in oral and written language.

14. Learning should stem from curiosity and interest, while enthusiasm should be capitalized upon.

15. Students need direct experiences where they learn to experiment, to make discoveries, and to create and test hypotheses.

16. Students need to be taught to be independent and to think for themselves, while learning to make wise choices, and becoming self-directed learners.

17. Critical and creative thinking processes must be included in each child's day, along with experiences with higher level thinking activities.

18. Students will need to be taught the processes and skills that will enable them to communicate effectively with others.

19. Skills related to science, social studies, and math will also need to be presented as a major part of the program.

20. The classroom environment will need to include emphasis on success for every student, with continuous growth for all.

"Emphasis must be on success for every student, with continuous growth for all."

ADVICE FROM THE EXPERTS

"The less we expect kids to be the same, the more they will respect and enjoy the differences among them. When that type of atmosphere is achieved, kids are free to learn from each other, and teachers have more time to teach."
Jane Mitchell
"Two Grades are Better Than One"

"The process is more important than the product. The skills of learning to learn, especially inquiry, evaluation, interpretation, synthesis, and application are stressed."
Robert H. Anderson and Barbara N. Pavan
Nongradedness: Helping It to Happen

"All children can learn, if the school environment is conducive to promoting success at all times."
Edmonds Nongraded Staff
The Edmonds Project

"There is a strong positive relationship between the ability to think critically, to perform higher-order thinking and to think more creatively when learning occurs in group settings."
James Bellanca and Robin Fogarty
Blueprints for Thinking in the Cooperative Classroom

OVERVIEW OF ORGANIZATION

Create multi-age family units.

◊ Create classrooms with teachers, parents, and students who believe in the philosophy of multi-age instruction.

◊ Develop a family atmosphere by having close contact between home and school, and by getting to know each student well.

◊ Let students know you care about them and their progress.

Combine two to three grade levels.

◊ It may be advisable to start with two grade levels if you are just beginning a multi-age program. At some point, however, you might want to consider keeping those students and picking up a younger group to combine with them.

It is easier to start a program with two grade levels, however, the group dynamics with three grade levels is even more conducive to continuous progress and greater acceleration of students. Younger students will gain from the exposure to higher-level work and from participating in discussions with students who are able to handle more difficult material.

◊ Give children opportunities to be role models for the younger students, or to look up to role models among the older students.

Leadership skills are developed as students have a chance to be led by the older students, then take their own turns leading the younger students.

◊ Cultivate friendships between children of different ages.

Valuable relationships can be developed between children of different ages, which will carry over to other aspects of their lives.

Use heterogeneous groupings.

◊ Assign students who are as different as possible, with varying personalities, interests, and behaviors.

> *Be careful not to set up a class that is mainly less able older students together with more mature or brighter younger students. This can lead to poor self-concepts among the older students, and the younger students do not have the advantage of learning from the older students.*

◊ It is essential to have students of all ability levels from each age group, in order for group dynamics to be the best that they can be.

Eliminate grade level designations.

◊ Do not refer to students by grade levels, and ask students to not refer to each other by grade levels.

◊ Think of and treat the entire class as a group of students from a multi-age range.

> *It improves the classroom atmosphere when all of the children feel that they are just part of a group assigned to a certain classroom, and that what age they are is not important.*

◊ Assign students to work with different-aged students throughout the day, and expect them to consider each other as classmates, without regard to age.

◊ Explain to the class that younger students are just as likely to be helping older students as vice versa, depending on who happens to know the most about a topic.

Provide continuous growth through developmental levels.

◊ Assign work to students according to developmental levels, without regard to age or predetermined grade levels.

◊ Diagnose the needs of each individual, then provide instruction for continuous growth, according to those needs.

Maintain two-teacher teams.

◊ Team teaching is a very important part of this type of instruction.

> _Due to the wider range of activities needed, it is especially helpful to share your expertise and responsibilities with another teacher._

◊ If you cannot work with a team partner, you can still run a multi-age class, but you should try to work closely with another multi-age teacher and support each other's efforts.

◊ When possible, teacher teams should consist of teachers with experience on different grade levels.

> _This will make planning and teaching easier, as you will have a wider range of experience and resources from which to draw ideas._

"Diagnose the needs of each individual, then provide instruction for continuous growth."

Keep students with the same teachers for two to three years.

◊ Less review and diagnosis time will be needed at the beginning of every year as teachers will already know where many of their students are.

Time usually spent becoming acquainted with students is cut down. The teacher will begin working with children on their own levels sooner than usual, as returning students will basically start where they left off the year before, with less review. The teacher will be able to concentrate on the new students in the class and will get to know them sooner.

◊ Returning students will know your expectations and classroom rules, so less time needs to be spent on these at the beginning of the year.

Older students will help younger students to learn these expectations. They will help the younger students to understand what you consider as acceptable behavior.

◊ Keeping students for two or three years with the same teacher team helps to build a family atmosphere.

Rapport is improved by knowing students and their parents better. Closer relationships develop as a result of this rapport, which tend to help cut down on discipline problems. This close relationship between home and school helps to create a family atmosphere.

Provide common planning times.

◊ Teachers who are teaming really need to have as many common planning times as possible. Extra time for team partners to meet and plan will be necessary.

This is especially true with multi-age instruction, as you will be designing more of your own curriculum. More time will be needed to work with your partner to make decisions about your classroom.

◊ If team planning time is tied to specialists, such as P.E. and music, try to schedule so that half of your class goes to one specialist at the same time that the other half of the class meets with another specialist.

Set up double classrooms called centers, preferably with open walls between them.

◊ When possible, set up two classrooms that have walls that are open or can be opened.

If these are not available, ask for permission to have openings cut between adjoining rooms. Removing about a third of an adjoining wall may be ideal, because then you can have two large teaching stations, one on each side. This way, teachers can teach without distracting each other, but can still see most of what is happening in both rooms when standing where they can see through the opening. There will be times when both teachers will be working with students in the same classroom and will need to be able to supervise the opposite classroom, by at least having a view of the children working there.

◊ Another possibility is to have two rooms completely opened up so that they are one large classroom.

Some teaching partners prefer to teach this way as they feel more like one large group, with two teachers. At times, with this configuration, noisy activities on one side of the room can be distracting to the rest of the room. This needs to be considered, as it is important to have some quiet areas somewhere in your center. If you use a large room, try dividing the room into smaller sections by screening, or using free standing blackboards or bookcases as partitions.

Place two groups of students in each center.

◊ Assign students to a double center, not to individual teachers.

◊ Both teachers should work with all children so that the children actually have two teachers instead of one.

You may find that some students tend to develop a closer relationship with one teacher than the other. We all know some students that we don't feel as close to as others, and yet another teacher might be able to develop a great rapport with them. It helps teachers to see these students through the eyes of another teacher.

Set up flexible classroom environment--tables, couches, pillows, etc.

◊ Change your classroom environment from the way a traditional classroom looks.

> _Use tables, if possible, large enough for at least four students to work. If you cannot get tables, then at least put desks together in groups. Ask parents for couches, stuffed chairs, floor pillows, small rugs, etc. Many of them will have items they are willing to donate to your classroom._

◊ Design your classroom environment according to your needs.

> _Be aware of such things as where the sinks are located, where the outlets are, where storage areas are, etc. You will need a teaching area near a blackboard. You will need areas for supplies such as math manipulatives, science equipment, social studies materials, art supplies, etc. Your library will need to be in a quiet corner. There should be an area to display student work. Storage areas for student supplies and portfolios should be accessible to students._

"Design your classroom environment according to your needs."

12

Create learning centers.

◊ Set up learning centers with equipment out and handy for children to explore.

◊ Gather ideas to post at learning centers that can be used at any time. They don't necessarily have to fit your current theme, or the unit your instruction is currently based on.

Science, math, social studies, and art especially lend themselves to hands-on materials that can be left out at all times so children can use them when they have the time to do so, even if they do not have a definite assignment.

◊ Find a quiet corner for a reading and writing center.

Stock this center with plenty of materials to read and lots of writing supplies and ideas for what to write about. Students can store reading and writing folders in these centers and obtain them as they are needed.

Provide areas for whole group instruction and planning. (See pp. 68-71 for scheduling of a typical day.)

◊ Set aside an area where all of your students can sit, preferably on the floor or an area where they can bring just their chairs to sit and listen to instruction or directions.

This will be where children gather first thing in the morning for a meeting, where they will plan their day. Announcements can be given, attendance can be taken, teachers and students can share, films and videos can be shown, etc. You may also wish for students to end the day in this area as they discuss and evaluate their day and plan for the next day.

DAILY SCHEDULE
9:10 Morning Meeting   1:00 Centers
9:30 Theme Choice   2:15 Recess
10:30 Recess   2:30 Art
10:45 Math Menus   3:15 Clean-up
12:00 Lunch Recess   3:30 Dismissal

13

RESULTS OF ORGANIZATIONAL CHANGES

Students will progress at their own pace and many of them will be accelerated. They will learn to work more cooperatively and have better self esteem. Children will develop closer relationships with teachers and will socialize with students of different ages, looking up to role models they can follow. They will feel successful as they make continuous progress without failure. Students will receive recognition, regardless of their ability. They will gain in self-confidence.

Teachers will become facilitators for classroom activities and will use a greater variety of instructional strategies. They will grow in expertise in areas of their choice as they share responsibilities with team members. Teacher partners will choose and write curriculum according to student needs and will have a greater awareness of individual needs. They will become comfortable with many different types of grouping patterns. They will develop closer relationships with students and parents.

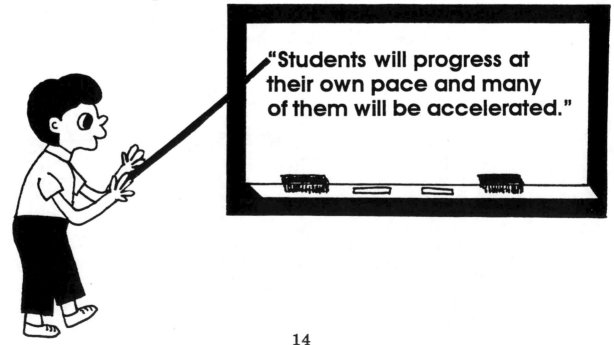

"Students will progress at their own pace and many of them will be accelerated."

ADVICE FROM THE EXPERTS

"There is agreement that if children are with other children who are academically inclined, they'll more easily get what they need academically and that multiage family groupings are one way of causing this to happen."
Charles Rathbone, Anne Bingham, Peggy Dorta, Molly McClaskey, Justine O'Keefe
Multiage Portraits: Teaching and Learning in Mixed-age Classrooms

"Students in a multi-age classroom learn that everyone has ability and can demonstrate competence in some area. Self-direction and independence are developed."
Bruce Miller
The Multigrade Classroom: A Resource Handbook for Small Rural Schools

"Cooperative learning should be used whenever teachers want students to learn more, like school better, like each other better, have higher self-esteem, and learn more effective social skills."
David Johnson and Roger Johnson
Learning Together and Alone

"One benefit of teachers working together is that they can draw on each other's strengths. But perhaps the greatest personal benefit to any teacher wanting to try something innovative is that of having a supportive partner, someone with whom to share the frustrations and successes of trying something new."
Jim Grant and Bob Johnson
A Common Sense Guide to Multiage Practices

OVERVIEW OF INSTRUCTIONAL STRATEGIES

Facilitate learning of individuals.

◊ Become a facilitator instead of a whole class instructor.

◊ Turn students loose on small group and individual activities whenever possible, and then spend your time helping individual groups of students while they are working.

> *This organization gives you much more time to help the students who really need you, while working with individual students at their correct developmental levels.*

Stress small group and individualized instruction.

◊ Your goal should be to have children working in small cooperative groups as much as possible, or on individual assignments.

> *Even if the whole class is working on the same assignment, try to use cooperative learning groups with peer tutoring, as children who require help need as much of this type of experience as possible.*

◊ It is not necessary for children to always be graded on daily assignments, so it doesn't matter which student finds the answer.

> *It is much more beneficial for children to work together on assignments and help each other with answers, so that everyone finds the right answer and understands the assignment. Children do not tend to just copy answers in these situations, but show each other where the answers are.*

Provide some whole group instruction.

◊ There are still times for whole group instruction, including your double-sized group.

   This instruction is more likely to be at the beginning of units or projects when you are orienting students with overviews of what is ahead of them. Short lessons including information that all students need to know can sometimes be given to the whole group in lecture form.

◊ Some hands-on science lessons or social studies lessons may lend themselves to whole class instruction due to the necessary teacher involvement.

◊ When you are first starting you will use more whole group instruction, but look for ways to get beyond it as soon as possible.

"There are still times for whole group instruction."

Mainstream special needs students.

◊ There are advantages when special needs students are placed in multi-age classrooms.

> *Because students are working on so many different levels within the classroom, students who need more help or are working below grade level are not as obvious to others as they usually would be.*

◊ Peer tutoring is especially helpful to the special needs student.

> *More help is available in a multi-age classroom than just what the teacher can provide. As special needs students have a chance to work with regular students, they gain from the knowledge of their peers as well as from teacher instruction. They do not have this advantage if they are segregated from their peers.*

Use remediation specialists working in classrooms.

◊ Remediation specialists are most helpful working in the classroom with students who need extra help.

> *Students will obtain more help with regular classroom work if specialists work in the classroom, helping with the assignments that the classroom teacher has given to them. By working closely with the teacher, the specialist can be more aware of what each student needs to be successful in a particular classroom.*

◊ Pull outs of remediation students are not recommended.

> *Students are more likely to feel positive about accepting help if it is in their own classroom, as many of them are embarrassed by being pulled out to work with a remedial teacher. When the specialists work in the room, sometimes including other students that need help but did not qualify for special help, the special needs student does not stand out as needing extra attention. This helps to increase self-esteem.*

Guide learning by establishing scope and sequence.

◊ Your job will be to guide your students through a scope and sequence of activities, with emphasis on the placement of each child along a continuum.

◊ You will need to know where children are and help them to see where they are headed.

"You will need to know where children are and help them to see where they are headed."

Obtain materials and place them where children can find them.

◊ Gather materials and supplies children will need and find places for them that are centrally located or in different centers.

Children need to find these supplies by themselves without bothering you. They need to be taught where supplies are, how to use them, and to put them back where they belong when finished using them.

Guide students working cooperatively in pairs or in teams.

◊ Teach students how to work cooperatively in pairs or teams.

◊ Guide students to be more effective team members by showing them what is expected and setting goals for group work.

◊ Do not allow children to come to you if anyone in their group knows answers to their questions.

If children are taught how to work cooperatively, they will learn to find answers for themselves or with the help of friends.

Use different grouping configurations. (See p. 72 for grouping strategies.)

◊ Achievement grouping may be used when children with the same needs are called together to work on skills.

◊ Interest grouping may be used when students are interested in the same topics.

◊ Heterogeneous grouping may be used when you want students of different abilities or interests to be working together on projects.

◊ Homogeneous grouping may be used to form instructional groups when children have similarities that you want to focus on.

◊ Random grouping may be used when it doesn't matter what the interests or abilities of group members are.

All of these groupings should be flexible and changed often.

"Guide students to be more effective team members by showing them what is expected and setting goals for group work.

Change grouping configurations throughout the day.

◊ Students should be grouped differently throughout the day so that each child has a chance to work with every other child in the classroom at some time.

◊ P.E. and music groups should be different than thematic groups. Novel groups and math groups should be different than P.E. and music groups, etc.

It adds to socialization skills and is motivating and stimulating to children to work with different individuals throughout the day instead of staying in the same place with the same peers.

Use learning centers for small group work or individual work.

◊ Use as many self-directed activities as possible and rotate children through learning centers.

◊ Individuals and small groups can locate needed materials and work independently while you monitor progress.

Emphasize peer tutoring.

◊ Train children to work together and to help each other with projects as needed.

Children gain from teaching concepts to others as well as by having other children help them. This will not always be the older child helping the younger one, but rather the one who knows the most about a particular topic will help explain concepts to others. Self esteem is enhanced by being able to explain material to other students.

◊ Students who need help get immediate feedback from peers that you cannot possibly give to each individual. More learning goes on with this teaching strategy.

Stress peer evaluation.

◊ Teach children to evaluate each other during group times.

> *They can proofread for each other and help each other edit written material. They can show each other mistakes and explain corrections. They can praise peers for doing a good job or creating an interesting presentation.*

◊ Students will appreciate knowing that other students are interested in their work and care about them.

Utilize research for gaining knowledge.

◊ Become research-oriented in your planning.

> *Plan as many activities for children as possible where they will do research to find answers, gain information, or solve problems.*

◊ Teach students how to do research correctly.

> *They need to learn how to take notes, write rough drafts, proofread, and write final papers. This is a skill that takes a lot of instruction and practice. If students are to become independent learners, they must develop these skills to the fullest.*

AUTHOR'S NOTE
SEE MY BOOK DEVELOPING RESEARCH SKILLS, CATS PUBLICATIONS, 1995, ON TEACHING CHILDREN HOW TO DO RESEARCH. LESSONS INCLUDED PROVIDE STUDENTS WITH EXPERIENCE IN NOTE TAKING, FOLLOWING OUTLINES, WRITING ROUGH DRAFTS, PROOFREADING, AND COMPLETING FINAL REPORTS. PAGES ARE READY TO BE REPRODUCED FOR STUDENT USE.

Use parent volunteers.

◊ Take advantage of parents who are willing to come in to help with teaching small groups and individuals.

Train parents to help with instruction and not just clerical work. They can be very helpful supervising learning centers and individual projects.

◊ Remember to let parents know what you are studying, what your themes are, etc.

Some of your parents may have an interest or expertise in an area you are covering, that they would be willing to share with students.

"Parents can be very helpful supervising learning centers and individual projects."

Train older students as volunteers.

◊ Older students from other classrooms, especially those who have been in your classroom, can be very helpful in supervising and tutoring your students.

The relationships that develop between the ages are very special. Your students will really look up to the older students as role models. It is also a very special experience for the older student to be considered as a role model by your students.

Give students choice in learning activities.

◊ Your classroom should be built around choice activities.

> *Not only should children have a choice about what they will learn, but they should also have a choice as to how they will learn it.*

◊ Let students help you decide what to include in your curriculum.

◊ Give students a choice as to what their day will look like.

> *If students can schedule when they will work on certain activities, they will follow their moods and learning styles and work more efficiently on what they feel like doing at different times of the day.*

> *Some students may choose to spend a double period or a longer time on a project that is especially important to them, or something they consider a priority to finish. They will make more progress when they are allowed to do so.*

◊ Letting students follow their interests and talents, and decide how they will learn certain concepts, allows for greater appreciation of what is to be learned.

Use inquiry methods for science instruction.

◊ Give children many experiences with inquiry, building hands-on experiences into your curriculum.

◊ Let them seek solutions and solve problems for themselves instead of just teaching them facts.

> *Children will learn more when they have a chance to think and predict what is going to happen before they do experiments.*

24

RESULTS OF INSTRUCTIONAL STRATEGY CHANGES

Students will display more interest in school activities and will be further motivated for learning. They will have a greater curiosity and will show greater development in areas of strength. They will exhibit a stronger desire to cooperate, due to increased interaction with peers, and will demonstrate better empathy and understanding of others.

Children willl demonstrate enhanced development in self-discipline and dependability and will accept some of the responsibility for their own learning. They will become self-directed and goal-oriented. They will become better time managers, and will be more likely to complete work on time. They will show increased attendance.

Research skills will be developed and students will learn more due to increased exposure to higher level material, different methods of instruction, and their understanding of learning styles. Students will have a more positive attitude toward school, toward each other, and toward learning.

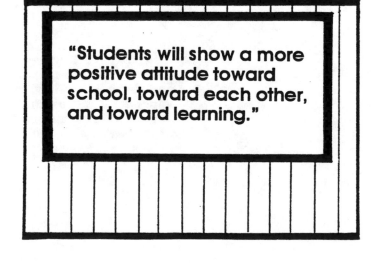

"Students will show a more positive attitude toward school, toward each other, and toward learning."

ADVICE FROM THE EXPERTS

"Teachers are facilitators of learning. They aid in
childrens' development by helping them to formulate
goals and diagnose problem areas. They suggest
alternative plans of action, provide resource materials,
and give encouragement or support or prodding as needed."
Robert H. Anderson and Barbara N. Pavan
Nongradedness: Helping It to Happen

"We must keep children with educational
problems in heterogeneous classrooms.
The specialists should help teachers
in the classrooms."
Dr. William Glasser
Schools Without Failure

"Many students may learn better from their
peers than from adults, and many students
benefit greatly from teaching other students."
David Johnson and Roger Johnson
Learning Together and Alone

"Individual differences in the pupil
population are accepted and respected,
and there is ample variability in instructional
approaches to respond to varying needs."
Robert H. Anderson and Barbara N. Pavan
Nongradedness: Helping It to Happen

OVERVIEW OF CURRICULUM

Integrate the subject areas.

◊ As many of the subject areas as possible should be integrated.

> *Research says that children learn more when subjects are integrated, as they can see the relationships between them. In real life we don't find isolated problems and situations. We learn to use all of our resources to solve problems. Keeping the subjects isolated does not reflect reality as we know it. We need to see the connections.*

◊ Restraints of time blocks should be eliminated by not considering each subject a separate entity.

> *Activities can run as long as needed when subjects don't have to fit into set time blocks. Children will have time to explore topics more deeply. They will also have more time to pursue their interests and follow their talents.*

◊ Integration of subjects also helps the problem of never finding the time to teach everything you're expected to teach.

> *There just is not enough time in the school day to cover everything when subjects are all taught separately.*

"Children will have the time to explore topics more deeply when the subjects are integrated"

Use interdisciplinary curriculum.

◊ The teacher should consciously tie more than one subject together for students so that they can examine a problem, an issue, a theme, an experience, etc. from different disciplines.

> *When subjects are tied together in this way, the student day becomes less fragmented, and more time can be spent on one topic. This is particularly motivating and stimulating for children as they don't usually like having to stop in the middle of an activity that they are absorbed in just because the period is over.*

◊ Children will need to be taught the connections between subjects.

◊ Whenever possible, children should have a chance to plan part of the curriculum according to their interests, abilities, and learning styles.

◊ Disciplines such as art, music, and physical education should be part of the curriculum design.

Create thematic units. (See pp. 82-84 for thematic projects.)

◊ Consider setting a theme for the entire year that can be broken into separate units, or following different themes for shorter periods of time.

> *Working with thematic units is very motivating for students. Themes that teachers choose are usually more closely related to children's lives and are more interesting to them than subject material covered when subjects are taught in isolation.*

◊ Choose a theme that is broad enough that you can incorporate all of the subjects.

> *You may want to use webbing to take a look at a theme to see if it is worth developing. Think of what knowledge you will want students to have and decide on the main concepts you will cover. Dig for resources for children to use and think of possible activities including all of the disciplines.*

◊ Write inquiries for students to complete which vary in levels of difficulty.

Follow interests and abilities of students.

◊ Consider your individual students when deciding on themes.

> *Ask yourself: What are their interests and abilities?
> What type of material can they handle? What do they
> already know? How independent are they? How much help
> do they need while working? If your students had a choice to
> follow their passions, what would they want to study? What
> would they want to learn more about? How would they want
> to learn? What types of inquiries would they be interested in?*

Accommodate learning styles, brain dominance and multiple intelligences.

◊ Be sure to show and tell students what to do when you
plan lessons.

> *Your visual and auditory learners will pick up
> more on one than the other. Don't forget the tactile /
> kinesthetic learners. Activities must also be provided for
> those that don't learn well visually and / or auditorily.*

◊ Remember to be aware of light and sound.

> *Where should activities be held in your classroom?
> Quiet areas will be needed for some students. You may even
> use headphones for them to use as noise breakers.*

◊ Consider the time of day that you plan for different activities.

> *Vary the time that you spend on the same activity on
> different days in order to give morning and afternoon people
> quality time on each activity.*

◊ Consider the children who need some time working by
themselves.

> *There will be some children who will prefer
> to work alone, and there should be some times when this is
> possible for these children, at the same time that you are
> encouraging group configurations.*

◊ Be aware of children who need food during the day.

> *Give students a chance to bring in healthy food for snacks if they want to. After a few days of having this option, you will find that only the ones that really need intake during the day will bring food. They can find a time to have a small snack without disturbing others and most will just continue working while they eat.*

◊ Be sure to build in movement when you are planning units.

> *Some of your students just cannot sit still for long, and if they are free to get up and move from place to place at times, you will have fewer problems with the hyperactive child.*

◊ Use learning styles inventories.

> *Determine whether students are concrete sequential, abstract random, abstract sequential, or concrete random in learning styles. You should find out what your teaching style is. It is especially important to be aware of activities for the students who do not learn the same way you do.*

"It is especially important to be aware of activities for the students who do not learn the same way you do."

◊ Include right brain and left brain activities.

> *Activities need to be varied so that children who are left or right brain dominant have a chance to learn in the way that is natural for them, but also strengthen the other side of the brain.*

◊ Plan for the multiple intelligences of children.

> *Include activities of each type, according to "Gardner's Theory of Multiple Intelligences." Students should have the opportunity to process information in seven different ways. Provide activities that are logical-mathematical, linguistic, musical, spatial, bodily-kinesthetic, interpersonal, and intrapersonal.*

Use children's literature for language instruction.
(See pp. 85-86 for management using novels for instruction.)

◊ Build your classroom library, concentrating on having a great number of books. If you have enough, you will be able to build your language program around them.

> _Children are very motivated when their reading instruction comes from a variety of literature instead of from basal readers, as they have more choice in deciding what they will be reading._

◊ There are many different ways to use literature in your classroom.

> _Students may be reading in different novels, or small groups may be reading the same novel. Look at student objectives and develop lessons that can be used with any novel. Look at novels and build lessons that fit just that novel. There are many novel kits and idea packets on the market today to help with instruction using novels._

◊ Give students time to read good literature each day and read good literature to them.

> _Lessons can be built around what students read and also what you read. Reading aloud to students exposes them to good literature and helps them to appreciate it._

AUTHOR'S NOTE
    SEE MY BOOK <u>CREATIVE PROJECTS FOR INDEPENDENT LEARNERS,</u> CATS PUBLICATIONS, 1995. INCLUDED YOU WILL FIND MANY IDEAS RELATING TO USING LITERATURE WITH CHILDREN. PROJECTS ARE DESIGNED TO HELP THE TEACHER USE NOVELS FOR READING INSTRUCTION, WITH SPECIAL EMPHASIS ON DEVELOPING COMPREHENSION SKILLS AND HIGHER-LEVEL THINKING SKILLS.

Emphasize the writing process, whole language.

◊ Stress writing as a major part of a student's day.

> *Students' learning to express themselves in writing is an important part of this type of instruction. As students may often be working on different projects, they will also learn a great deal from each other by reading what other students have written.*

◊ The whole language approach, where children read, write, spell, listen, and speak about what they are learning in all areas, should be a major emphasis.

◊ Teach children the writing process.

> *They do not have to go through all the steps with each piece of writing, but they do need to understand all of the steps and become proficient with each step.*

Use basals as supplements.

◊ A collection of different basal readers can still be valuable in the classroom.

◊ As long as basal readers are not used as the basis for reading instruction, they can serve several different purposes.

> *There are many stories in these books that will correspond to your thematic units. You may find stories or tales from different countries you are studying. There may be science and social studies type articles that fit your units. There may be stories that children want to read that fit their interests that have nothing to do with your theme. There may be skills lessons that fit what your students need to learn.*

◊ You do not need a whole set of any of the basals. It would be much more helpful to have smaller numbers of several different sets, on different levels, to give you the variety that you will be looking for.

Provide self-pacing, self-directed activities.

◊ Look for self-pacing, self-directed activities on all levels.

> *Children will need to spend time working on these types of activities in order to be working on their own individual levels.*

◊ You will probably have to write some of these activities yourself, but there are commercial kits for reading, math, language, science, and social studies that are self-pacing, with work on different levels.

"Provide self-directed activities that promote continuous progress."

Promote continuous individual progress.

◊ Your goal should be to promote continuous progress for each individual.

> *If work is truly at the right level for each individual, this goal should be accomplished. The use of self-pacing materials on the correct developmental levels will help you to see where children are and to see that they are progressing through the levels.*

◊ It is also important for you to do your best to see that children are working up to potential in all areas in the classroom.

◊ Lessons must be on the appropriate developmental levels for each individual.

> *This does not mean that every child needs to have a separate assignment. All students can be given the same assignment at times. With choice built into your lessons, and lessons that include projects on different developmental levels, children will be able to choose activities that fit their correct levels. You may need to guide them to do so, but be sure to set high expectations for your students, and let them know what you feel they are capable of doing.*

Stress creative and critical thinking.

◊ Teaching students to think for themselves should be one of your main goals.

◊ Thematic instruction gives you a chance to help develop creative thinking as children work with several different disciplines at the same time.

> *Help children to put ideas together and come up with new ideas or unique approaches to learning. Give them lots of chances to solve problems in creative ways.*

◊ Build in critical thinking activities that ask students to make judgments on what they believe or do.

> *Children need to spend time reasoning and reflecting on material and learning to think logically and objectively.*

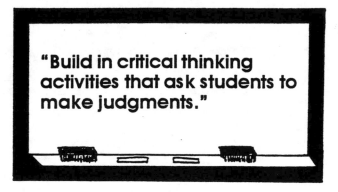

"Build in critical thinking activities that ask students to make judgments."

Emphasize higher level thinking skills.
(See pp. 73-81 for instructions on using Bloom's Taxonomy.)

◊ Teach children the different levels of thinking.

> *Have students practice writing questions on the different levels. They can understand the levels when they are taught the different process verbs and how to use them.*

◊ Be sure that you are writing inquiries for the children that include higher level thinking.

Include typing and keyboarding instruction.
(See p. 54 for suggestions on obtaining typewriters.)

◊ Supply children with typewriters and give them lessons on keyboarding.

Even young children can learn how to type as soon as their hands are big enough to fit the keyboard. In this day of computers, it is essential that children learn keyboarding skills. They will make much more progress with word processing if they know the keyboard.

AUTHOR'S NOTE: Excellent programs for keyboarding instruction, with student typing guides and videos are available from Joyful Noise Publications, Edmonds, WA. For information, call (425) 774-7078.

Teach word processing skills.

◊ Provide time for children to learn word processing skills.

Initialize a disk for each student and let students practice word processing skills whenever they can.

◊ Guide students to type reports, spelling lists, short stories, or whatever else they are working on.

Students will be able to save whatever they write in this way and the disks should become part of their portfolios at the end of the year. This is a great way to show progress in writing and in word processing skills.

Work with the latest in technology.

◊ Learn as much as you can about technology and teach as much as possible to your students.

Children should all become computer literate. They should learn to operate video recorders, video cameras, laser disk machines, CD Rom players, and / or whatever you have access to for them to use.

Include foreign language instruction.

◊ Learn a foreign language and teach it to your students, even as you are learning it.

Children pick up quickly on foreign languages, and research says they will learn more if they learn while they are young. Many books, tapes, videos, etc. are available for use in foreign language instruction.

Do not be afraid to learn along with students if you are not proficient in a foreign language. This involvement on your part is of great value to them.

"Learn a foreign language and teach it to your students, even as you are learning it."

RESULTS OF
CURRICULUM CHANGES

Students will feel successful in all areas of growth. They will be more mature and will be able to make wise choices and decisions. They will progress at a faster rate through the curriculum, as they make continuous progress, and will be able to solve problems for themselves. They will know their own learning styles and strengths and will choose activities that are appropriate. They will be able to use both oral and written language more effectively.

Children will have experience with word processors and will be able to do their own typing. They will begin speaking a foreign language. They will have a greater appreciation for the arts. Teachers will see greater student growth in dependability, responsibility, and independence, as children have increased interest and motivation.

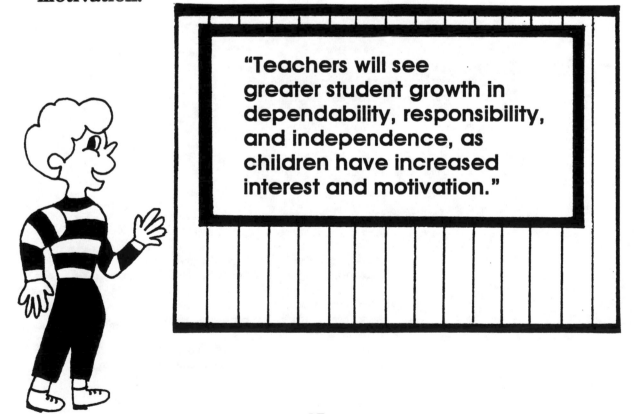

"Teachers will see greater student growth in dependability, responsibility, and independence, as children have increased interest and motivation."

ADVICE FROM THE EXPERTS

"Teaching with themes or concepts that cut across traditional curriculum areas offers a flexibility that allows children of different ages and abilities to become involved and to learn at their own pace."
Jim Grant and Bob Johnson
A Common Sense Guide to Multiage Practices

"The integrated day is a natural day. Time is structured according to the needs of the students, and the needs of the curriculum are planned around them. Motivation is often high with this approach because the areas of study are directly linked to children's lives. Students can and, when possible, should be involved in the development of interdisciplinary units."
Heidi Hayes Jacobs
Interdisciplinary Curriculum: Design and Implementation

"The teacher has power, competence, and commitment in designing an environment rich in ideas, topics, and materials to stimulate and guide independent learning and success."
Dr. Roger Taylor
Using Integrated, Thematic Teaching Strategies to Increase Student Achievement and Motivation

"Higher level thinking is enhanced when members of a group learn to listen, value each member's unique contribution, take another person's point of view, engage in a variety of group roles, achieve consensus, and resolve conflicts."
James Bellanca and Robin Fogarty
Blueprints for Thinking in the Cooperative Classroom

OVERVIEW OF
ASSESSMENT and
EVALUATION

Report each individual's growth according to potential.

◊ Report on the individual development of children.

> _It is important to know where each child is and what potential each child has, then report to parents according to the growth being demonstrated as compared to potential._

◊ Praise children for any growth they demonstrate if they are working hard, even if they have not moved very far.

"It is important to know where each child is and what potential each child has."

Assess and evaluate mastery of learning objectives.

◊ Use a mastery approach and allow children to make continuous progress by allowing them to move on as they master objectives.

◊ Let students know what you will be evaluating, and assess them continually as they are working, so that you will know when they are ready to move ahead.

Consider eliminating all letter grades, and use promotions and retentions only when developmentally appropriate.

◊ If your district will allow, eliminate all letter grades.

> *Evaluate students according to potential and not in comparison to arbitrary standards for a particular grade level. Use narrative to report on student growth.*

◊ Keep a child in your multi-age class for an extra year if it is developmentally appropriate to do so.

> *If some children need a longer time to master the objectives, they may remain in your classroom for an extra period of time, but they should pick up where they left off, rather than having to repeat an entire year. With multi-age classes, the students will be with many of the same children again, and they are not as likely to feel as if they have failed.*
>
> *Remember, however, that children learn at different rates and some of the children who are progressing slowly will catch up with their peers after a period of time, especially if they move on in a multi-age environment. The strategies of cooperative learning and peer tutoring, and exposure to higher level material are very beneficial to these students.*

◊ It is also advisable not to promote children to a higher grade placement unless it is developmentally appropriate.

> *In most cases it is usually better for a child to remain with the same group of children as they progress for social and emotional reasons. If children are taught at the correct level and are making continuous progress, then there should be little need for promotion above grade levels. You will need to challenge each student at whatever level he or she needs to be working.*
>
> *It is possible that there will be a student, once in a while, that is more mature and developmentally ready in all growth areas to move on with a group of older children. He/she should have the opportunity to do so if the student, parents, and teachers all agree that this would be an appropriate placement.*

40

Eliminate comparisons of students to each other and to predetermined grade level objectives.

◊ Report individual progress according to mastery of objectives.

> *You should be reporting on where a child is along a continuum of objectives and not where the child supposedly should be for a certain grade level.*

◊ Report on progress made by each individual in all areas of growth.

> *Do not report on how children are doing in comparison to each other. Report on effort and achievement in each area according to the child's own potential and not in relation to other children.*

◊ Recognize that students learn at different rates.

> *All children can and will learn if they are picked up where they are and allowed to progress from that point. Just because a child is working more slowly at a given time does not mean that child will always be behind.*

"You should report individual progress in all areas of growth."

Develop and use a narrative system of reporting.

◊ Develop a report card of your own.

> *Use narrative to explain to children and parents the progress a child is making. This method is much more subjective and parents and students can get a better idea of where a student is.*

◊ Include strengths, weaknesses, and goals for improvement.

◊ Include all types of growth, not just academic, but also social, emotional, artistic, and physical.

Conduct at least one parent-teacher conference.

◊ Bring parents in for at least one parent-teacher conference.

It would be ideal if you could plan one in the fall and one in the spring.

◊ Explain your multi-age classroom and its structure.

This is another time to discuss with parents the different approach you are taking, then evaluate how their child is doing with this approach.

Include students in parent-teacher conferences.

◊ If possible, include your students in conferences.

You can have students there just for part of the conference if you feel you need to talk to a parent privately.

◊ Children in this type of classroom are taking a greater part in determining their own goals and plans for progress.

It is very worthwhile to let students explain to parents what they are doing and how they are progressing toward goals they have set.

Make students responsible for record keeping.
(See pp. 116-124 for record keeping forms.)

◊ Develop charts and graphs for children to use to show what independent work they are doing.

Such items as reading records, learning center records, assignment sheets, checklists, project records, etc. are more necessary when children are working individually.

◊ Students will need to accept responsibility for completing their own records.

It helps them to develop independence and responsibility when they keep their own records. They should keep their record sheets where you can see them at any time. They need to understand that they will not receive credit if they lose them, because you do not have a separate record.

Use student recognition programs.

◊ Recognize children for their accomplishments.

Children should be recognized for their efforts and for doing a good job at what is expected of them. They will appreciate being recognized for good work, and having it called to the attention of their peers. Be sure that __all__ students are recognized.

Help students set goals for their own performance.

◊ Help students to understand their own potential and to set reasonable goals for themselves.

Sometimes children will try to set goals that are too high. See that they set up goals in small steps so they will be easier to obtain, and they will receive recognition more often for doing so.

Teach students the characteristics of a good learner.
(See pp. 105-106 for ideas on using the learner characteristics.)

◊ Children need to be taught what it means to be a good learner.

They should know what it is that you expect of them and what characteristics you are looking for when you evaluate them.

◊ Zero in on one characteristic at a time and explain what it is that you think a child should do in order to reflect this characteristic.

Evaluate students on these learner characteristics.

◊ Evaluate children according to the characteristics that you have discussed with them.

If you have talked with them about increasing organizational skills, for instance, and they know what you think being organized means, then you should evaluate them according to what you have discussed. Children will make much more improvement if they understand how they are being evaluated.

Teach children to evaluate themselves on these characteristics.

◊ Children should look at themselves and at their work and evaluate it in the same way that you would.

They can make note of how they feel they did on assignments. They can write in journals to explain what kind of progress they think they are making.

Keep student portfolios with samples of student work.
(See pp. 109-111 with directions for using a portfolio system.)

◊ Each student should keep a portfolio, such as a scrapbook, in which work can be kept.

Daily work, tests, short stories, award certificates, art work, etc. should be collected and pasted into this portfolio.

◊ Teachers will have some input as to what goes into portfolios at times, but portfolios should be built around student choice.

Guide students to choose and evaluate their own contributions to portfolios.
(See pp. 112-115 for sample evaluation forms.)

◊ A child's portfolio should be a collection of work that the student is proud of, showing progress and accomplishments the student has made.

Most of the material that is included should be chosen by the student. You will need to guide your students to choose work that shows their ability and effort. You will also need to guide students to write evaluations to include next to work in their portfolios.

◊ Send portfolios home for parents to keep at the end of the year, or you may decide to keep them for more than one year, especially if you will have the same students again.

RESULTS OF ASSESSMENT AND EVALUATION CHANGES

Students will be more aware of the objectives they need to master, and will be able to keep their own records of performance. They will learn to assess and evaluate themselves and make choices for work to include in portfolios.

Students will understand how the teacher is evaluating them. They will take pride in their own accomplishments, then recognize and praise the efforts of others. Students will learn to set their own goals and will receive recognition for work that is well done.

"Students will learn to set their own goals and keep their own records of performance."

ADVICE FROM THE EXPERTS

"The multiage continuous progress program model acknowledges individual differences in rate of development, in ability, in learning styles. It is designed for a heterogeneous group of children and builds on that diversity."
Jim Grant and Bob Johnson
A Common Sense Guide to Multiage Practices

"Children with self-esteem are more enthusiastic, more willing to accept challenges, and more able to concentrate and to persevere."
British Columbia
Primary Program

"Students learn that they can count on their classmates to help when they need help, listen when they have something to contribute, and celebrate their accomplishments."
Susan E. Ellis and Susan F. Whalen
Cooperative Learning: Getting Started

"By evaluating learning through observation rather than relying primarily on tests, a teacher gets a much better understanding of the whole child and the many dimensions that affect that child's development."
Jim Grant and Bob Johnson
A Common Sense Guide to Multiage Practices

CONSIDERATIONS FOR
GETTING STARTED

Explain goals and changes to parents.

When a school staff has decided that multi-age classrooms are what they want for their school, parents must be notified and given a chance to find out what multi-age classrooms are all about. You must have their understanding and support before you attempt to make this kind of change.

Informational meetings should be held, preferably with a panel of experts or at least teachers who have taught this type of class successfully and/or principals who have had this type of experience. Literature on multi-age schools can also be reviewed and passed out at this time. After these meetings, parents should have choices to place children in this type of classroom if they wish to do so. It is best not to make this type of placement without the approval and full support of parents.

"It is best for teachers who have taught different grade levels to join together."

Start with teacher teams.

Team teaching is a very important component of a multi-age program. Whenever possible, it would be best for teachers who have been teaching different grade levels to join together. A greater variety of resources and experience on different levels will make the job easier for you when you start planning.

It is essential that the two teachers feel comfortable with each other, have similar beliefs and expectations for learners, and truly want to work as team members. A great deal of time will be spent together and both teachers will need to be understanding of each other and flexible. They must get along well, if they are going to be successful as a team.

47

Collect resources.

You will need to collect a greater variety of materials on different levels than you would need for a single-graded classroom. Materials for self-pacing and continuous progress may be something you don't already have. Be on the lookout for materials that can be used with any grade level, with different responses from children with varying abilities. Be sure to obtain many materials for independent research.

Build your novel collection and classroom library. Ask parents to send in books from home that they no longer care about. Go to used book stores, library book sales, garage sales, etc.

Find materials that can be used for extra-credit activities when children have spare time. A student should never be able to say, "I have nothing to do because I'm finished with everything." Provide ongoing assignments with a great variety of materials.

Set up multi-age classrooms.

Set up classrooms with materials, furniture, supplies, etc. that fit the ages of the children who will be in the class. Think about materials and furniture, keeping in mind the ages of the children and their amount of ability and independence.

Organize learning centers.

Set up your classroom with different areas for independent learning and small group instruction. These centers may be subject oriented, but it would be better if they were project oriented for thematic instruction units as soon as possible.

Some areas may be set aside throughout the year where children know they can find math manipulatives, science materials, globes, dictionaries, encyclopedias, etc. to be used whenever they are needed.

Diagnose students.

You will need to spend more time diagnosing students, in order to know exactly where each student is. In order to individualize instruction and provide materials for each student to make continuous progress, you will need to do more diagnosing than usual. Diagnose ability, interests, learning styles, etc. of each child.

Many different types of assessment and evaluation may be used for diagnosis. Standardized tests may be consulted, but informal testing is also very valuable to help you determine where children are. Observations of student work and behavior are just as important as written tests. Portfolios from earlier years would be of great value when assessing new students, if available.

Look for diagnostic materials that will give you an idea of where children are. Many short quizzes and tests come with basal readers. Tests from Weekly Reader and Scholastic News may also be of value. Inventories and other checklists can also help you to place your students in the correct levels for different lessons.

Math quizzes, dictation, spelling tests, writing samples, written summaries, etc. may all be used to help place children where they belong on a continuum of learning for each content area. Children will be placed differently for activities, depending on ability in different subjects. These placements will be changed regularly as you watch student progress. Students will be pulled out in small groups for many skills lessons, and will not be left with the same group for an extended period of time.

Work with support people.

Talk to support people such as music teachers, P.E. teachers, instructional materials specialists, remediation specialists, etc. about what you are doing. Enlist their help as you plan thematic units. They can add a great deal to what you are doing by following your themes and giving children experiences in their classes that correlate with what you are doing in your classroom.

Encourage specialists not to be fearful of your multi-age class, but to teach toward the higher level. If they use cooperative learning and peer tutoring, older or more able students will be very helpful in working with younger students to help them to understand activities. Younger students will also make great gains in these areas, if they are treated in this way. Remediation specialists are most valuable if they come into your classroom to work with students rather than pulling your students out of class.

Teach students to keep their own records of work accomplished.

Start right away teaching children how to keep track of assignments they are completing. If students are going to be working independently, at their own rate, they will need to accept responsibility for keeping accurate records of what they have completed. You will not need to be keeping separate records of work students do independently, if you can rely on students to do this for themselves.

Turn over as much of this responsibility as you can to your students. Let them know that on individualized self-pacing materials, for instance, they are the only ones keeping a record of what they are accomplishing. Stress the importance of this record being kept, faithfully and correctly, if they want credit for work completed.

Give students record-keeping forms and expect them to keep track of their own progress. (See pp. 116-124 for sample record-keeping forms.)

Students should be provided with record-keeping forms,and then given time to fill out these forms at the end of activities. Give them reading charts to keep track of how far they have read, assignment sheets with sections to check off as they finish assignments, research project and learning center progress reports, group evaluation forms, and daily schedules where they plan what to do for a day.

Students should put these forms in folders which are kept in a place where you can look at them, at any time, to see what progress a child has made. You should also meet with each child from time to time to discuss this progress and make note of it, for yourself.

"Make students responsible for keeping accurate records."

Set up a place where children can locate needed supplies and materials.

Classroom materials such as paper, scissors, glue, crayons, markers, staplers, staples, rulers, tape, etc. should be kept in a central location where children can find what they need without asking you for them. If you have several learning centers, you may want to have these materials available at each center.

50

Explain your expectations for students to share materials.

Students will need to understand the importance of taking care of materials they find around the room, as they will be expected to share with others. It is essential for them to do the best they can to keep materials together and try to keep parts of things from getting lost. They must be willing to share and not try to monopolize needed materials when working at centers or in small groups.

"Students will be expected to take good care of materials, and share them with others."

Have a definite place for students to turn in completed work.

This will be very important. Since students are not sitting in rows, with everyone doing the same assignment, you can't just have someone collect everyone's paper. Many different assignments will be going on at the same time and many of the assignments will be long term projects. Paper boxes with cubby holes, baskets, tubs, etc. labeled with project names rather than subjects, at times, will be helpful. These should remain stationary so children will always know what to do with papers.

It is not a good idea for students to just put papers on the teacher's desk. Keeping track of them would be very difficult, when children are working on many different assignments.

Have "cubbies" for students to use for keeping their own materials and supplies organized and handy.

Since students will not have their own desks but will be sitting at different desks or tables throughout the day, each student will need a "cubby", such as a plastic dishpan, a basket, etc. labeled with his/her name and placed somewhere in the room where items such as crayons, markers, glue, scissors, and extra paper can be kept.

Most of the students will carry notebooks around with them during the day but the "cubbies" need to be large enough for the notebooks to fit inside, as there are times when this will be necessary to get them out of the way of group activities.

Encourage students to keep their names on all of their belongings. They are likely to leave supplies behind in various places at the end of work periods, since they are not working at desks of their own. It is difficult to determine who these items belong to when they have not been put away, unless students have their names on them.

Help students to be organized, with a folder or a notebook section for each subject or project.

Organizational skills must be stressed with this type of program. Children will need to know where materials are at all times, and they can't just know that what they need is in their desk. When they are keeping materials in back packs and "cubbies" they will need to keep track of supplies they need.

It is essential that students have a folder or a notebook section for each subject or for each project they are working on. You should not be expected to hand out extra copies of lessons and directions. Students will need to accept the responsibility to keep these materials put away in the proper place where they can be found as needed.

"Students must learn organizational skills with this type of program."

Teach Bloom's Taxonomy to students. (See pp. 73-81 for activities using Bloom's Taxonomy.)

Teach the levels of Bloom's Taxonomy to students. Let them know that you are expecting them to progress through these levels as soon as they are capable of doing so. Teach them the process verbs that go with questioning strategies for the different levels. Have them answer questions on the different levels, but also teach them to write questions on the different levels using novels, short stories or science and social studies material.

It will be very necessary for students to understand Bloom's Taxonomy, if you are really going to be working with higher level thinking skills in your classroom.

Teach children how to evaluate themselves. (See pp. 103-108 for strategies using learner characteristics.)

Let children know what learner characteristics you are looking for. Let them know your expectations. Explain to them what you see and what you would like to see. Then teach them to evaluate themselves using these characteristics. It is also helpful to have children look for positive characteristics in each other and make note of them to tell you and to tell their classmates.

Obtain portfolios for each child. (See pp. 109-111 for directions on setting up a portfolio system.)

Find a scrapbook or staple large papers together for each child to use as a portfolio. Let the children decorate the covers and help them to understand that this will be a place where they can keep their best work, to show you and their parents what they are capable of doing. Each student should have a large part in deciding what is included in his/her portfolio. This should be a collection that a student is proud of, just like a portfolio that an artist might keep to show accomplishments.

There may be times when teachers will ask children to include certain materials that are not necessarily their best, but that can be used to show growth at a later date. Tests may need to be included.

Also consider the possibility of including computer disks with word processing activities, audio tapes of reading, reporting, etc., and/or video tapes showing work that a child has done in the classroom. These are wonderful representations of a child's work for a parent to keep, and parents are often willing to supply the needed tapes for their child.

Help children to determine their own learning styles.

Talk to your students about learning styles. Give them learning styles inventories so that you will know how each student learns best, but also see that each student is aware of the best way to learn. Encourage students to think of learning styles when they have choices for classroom activities.

Obtain typewriters, computers, and keyboarding programs.

Gather as many computers and as much software as you can, of course, but don't forget the possibility of children learning how to type on typewriters. There are many keyboarding programs that young students can learn to type from. Ask parents if they are willing to donate old electric typewriters to the classroom, or ask your high schools if they have any old ones they are ready to dispose of. This will free up time on the computers to be used for word processing, rather than just for learning how to type.

Enlist parent volunteers.

There are so many things that parents can do to help you in this type of classroom. Children need a lot of individual help and parents can be very valuable, especially if they come in regularly and know what you want them to do. They can listen to children read, grade papers, help children with editing, quiz children on facts, or help small groups or individuals with problem solving. The possibilities are endless.

Remember to consider the expertise and experiences of your parents. Many of them would like to come in and talk to your children or work with them on something they have a lot of knowledge about. Consider parent training programs where parents actually come in when the children are not there and meet with you while you explain how they can help you.

Parents who cannot come to school are often willing to help with clerical work at home, or they can trace and cut out bulletin board letters, grade papers, etc. Having parents help is a great way to keep communication going between home and school.

Parents are often very willing to go on field trips with you and if your school district allows it, using them as drivers instead of taking expensive school busses will give you more opportunities to take students on field trips.

Consider asking for voluntary donations.

Ask your parents to volunteer their time to your classroom, either by coming into the room to work or by working at home, if they can. You may also find that some of your parents are willing and able to make voluntary cash donations to your school. Talk to your principal, have your parent group discuss the possibilities, then poll your parent population to see if they are willing and able to try this. This should not be something that every parent is expected to do, as some of them can not spare the money, but you may find many others who could and would love to help. A fund can be set up, organized, and managed by your parent group.

This money can then be spent on extra computers, software, teaching materials, classroom supplies, extra novels, science and math supplies, etc. Classroom teachers may also be given portions of this extra money to spend as they see fit for whatever they need for classroom projects.

Be sure that your parent population knows there are other materials and supplies they might be able to donate, such as old books, games, and furniture. Be sure they understand that these would be appreciated as much as money.

ADVICE FROM THE EXPERTS

"Any school that wants to make nongradedness happen, can accelerate the process by adopting a team teaching approach working with multi-age pupil groups. Team teaching calls for teachers to work closely together in all dimensions of teaching, and to share responsibilities for aggregations of children."
Robert H. Anderson and Barbara N. Pavan
Nongradedness: Helping It to Happen

"The most important function of elementary education is to provide a variety of opportunities through which the learners develop skills and knowledge that will enable them to live and continue to learn in an ever-changing world."
Edmonds Nongraded Staff
The Edmonds Project

"The purpose of the school is to help the student to become the most fully actualized, happy, and productive person that he or she can become."
Dr. Roger Taylor
Using Integrated, Thematic Teaching Strategies to Increase Student Achievement and Motivation.

"Peer relationships are a critical element in the development and socialization of children. Constructive relationships with peers are a necessity. Cooperative learning activities help to enhance these relationships."
Roger Johnson, David Johnson, Edythe Holubec, Pat Roy
Circles of Learning: Cooperation in the Classroom

CLASSROOM ORGANIZATION: AREAS NEEDED

Teaching Stations

Areas for small group instruction with desks or tables for students to work at, preferably in front of blackboards, or in an area where an overhead projector screen is located.

Whole group planning area

A place, usually without tables and chairs, large enough for the entire group to gather for planning and directions.

Learning centers

Areas where self-pacing and independent work projects are laid out for students to work on. Each area may be devoted to a different subject, but some areas will most likely contain thematic work for current projects, where several subjects are integrated.

Quiet Area

A section of the classroom where quiet activities take place, for children who need to get away from more active learners.

Reading Corner

An area where library books are kept, preferably with couches, pillows, tables, chairs, etc., where children can read silently, or quietly to each other.

Research Area

A place where dictionaries, encyclopedias, thesauruses, atlases, almanacs, globes, etc. are kept. This should also include work tables where children can work on research projects.

Art Area

An area close to a sink, where art supplies can be obtained as needed for class projects. This area should also include books, charts, etc., with explanations for art projects students may complete independently.

Science Corner

An area where science supplies and materials are kept, as near to a sink as possible. This area should also include ideas for independent or extra-credit projects.

Math Corner

An area where math manipulatives and games are kept so that students may work as they have time to do so.

Supply Area

A place where scissors, staplers, staples, tape, paper, paper clips, markers, crayons, etc. are kept for students to use as needed.

Storage Area

A place to store tubs or "cubbies" in which students keep their personal belongings.

Writing-Workshop Area

An area where writing folders are kept so children can work on writing projects whenever they choose to do so. Daily logs and journals may also be kept in this area.

Computer Center

An area where students can work in order to learn word processing and other computer skills.

Typewriter Center

An area where students can work on keyboarding skills.

Teacher's Area

A location for the teacher's desk, supplies, manuals, etc.

Portfolio Storage Area

A place to keep student portfolios.

Game Area

An area to store classroom games so that children can find them as needed.

TECHNIQUES FOR CLASSROOM MANAGEMENT

1. Work with a team partner, if possible, or at least with another multi-age teacher.

◊ Start when and where you feel comfortable.

◊ You can not be expected to open up your classroom, all of a sudden, to individualized and small group instruction, learning centers, cooperative learning activities, etc.

◊ You will need to spend time planning together to determine management of activities and to decide what students will need to be taught before they are ready for this type of instruction.

2. Share responsibilities with your team member.

◊ As you plan and carry out these activities, be sure to share responsibilities.

◊ You can be of great help to each other by planning activities to be used with all students.

◊ Divide the responsibility for planning according to the expertise and interest of the team members, then feed off each other for more ideas.

◊ Do not just departmentalize, but put one teacher in charge of an activity and have the other teacher help with the planning and presenting of material.

◊ Group children and teach something twice, if necessary at times, but don't always present material in this way. Some activities lend themselves to whole group instruction, and teacher time does not always have to be used to teach a lesson twice when the two of you are able to handle the management and discipline of a double-sized group.

3. Open up your classroom slowly, as you and your students become ready.

◊ When you feel that you and your team member are ready to try small group activities, open up slowly by doing one activity at a time.

◊ Be sure students understand discipline expectations, and that you both agree on what those expectations are. It doesn't take the children long to figure out that one of you is more lenient than the other, if this is true. Some of them would love to play you against each other, just as they try to do with their parents.

4. Establish discipline expectations and classroom rules.

◊ Before you can start, just like in any class, discipline expectations must be explained to students. If students can help determine these expectations, they are more likely to follow your guidelines.

◊ Students will need to discuss and understand why self-discipline will be an important part of learning in this way. If they want the freedom to move around the room, they will need to accept the responsibility to stay on task, not bother others, and complete assignments on time.

CLASSROOM RULES
1. USE COMMON SENSE
2. TREAT EACH OTHER WITH RESPECT.
3. BE RESPONSIBLE FOR YOUR OWN BEHAVIOR.

5. Explain standards for group behavior.

◊ Spend time helping students to understand the dynamics of working with groups. Many children do not tend to be cooperative in group situations unless they are taught to be.

◊ Some students will need to develop respect for each other, learn to listen to group discussions, and give others a chance to participate. Some will need to learn to be contributing members and not just sit back and leave all of the work to others.

6. Teach students to be cooperative learners.

◊ Lists of expectations can be posted for children to see, such as:
1. Work cooperatively with your group.
2. Do your share of the work.
3. Listen to what others have to say.
4. Give everyone a chance to participate.
5. Complete your part of assignments on time.
6. Do not ask your teacher for help if anyone in your group can answer the question.

"Spend time helping students to understand the dynamics of working cooperatively in groups."

7. *Start early with activities in which children have to cooperate.*

◊ Set up several short activities where children work together. These activities should not be too difficult, and should be motivating so children will be likely to decide right away that it is fun to work together.

◊ Use a time period that gives students long enough to rotate with their group through several different activities.

◊ Procedures should be explained to students beforehand and some type of rotation pattern needs to be discussed so that children will know where to go when each time period is up. This should give children a chance to see that they need to get right down to work, then clean up and be ready to move to a different area for the next activity when told to do so. This type of procedure can be repeated until you feel children are ready to participate in longer projects.

8. *Have students evaluate group behaviors regularly.*
(See p. 124 for a group evaluation form.)

◊ If students are to work effectively in groups, they will need to be made aware of the dynamics of working together. They should evaluate the progress their group makes often.

◊ Names should not be used when students did not participate well, but behaviors that restricted group progress can be discussed, along with behaviors that made a group successful. Students can discuss the types of behaviors that they would like to see in their group the next time.

◊ Students who consistently do not behave well in groups should be left out of group work for a while until they are able to be contributing members.

"If students are to work effectively in groups, they will need to be made aware of the dynamics of working together."

9. Have students evaluate their own behavior in group situations.

◊ Students should evaluate their own contributions to group projects, then discuss how they feel they might improve the next time they work with a group, if necessary. This evaluation should be more private, as students who did not do well should not have to discuss it openly in front of group members.

10. Establish guidelines for working independently without bothering others.

◊ Students will need to know what is expected of them when they are working independently on individual projects. If they are to remain seated, work without talking, share materials, or work quietly with others, they need to understand your expectations.

◊ Students will need to be self-disciplined if you are going to be able to individualize instruction. They need to understand that you do not have time to spend correcting them, and that you expect them to be responsible for their own behavior.

11. Establish guidelines for using learning centers.

◊ Children need to be taught what is expected of them when they are using learning centers for instruction. They need to understand where to find materials, how to use them, and what to do with them when they are finished.

◊ Insist that children keep work areas clean and organized. Give them time to put materials away at the end of the period.

◊ It is essential that students leave a learning center in the same condition in which they found it.

12. *Give clear oral and written instructions for independent work.*

◊ If students are to work independently without bothering you, it is up to you to be sure that directions are understood.

◊ Instructions should be given orally and then written down on the blackboard or on instruction sheets for children to refer to, as necessary.

13. *Praise students and groups who are staying on task.*

◊ Praise for working hard, staying on task, and helping others needs to be given regularly. Students who do what is expected need to be recognized often for doing so.

◊ We, as teachers, tend to spend too much time noticing the disruptive behavior and forgetting to praise students who do what is expected of them.

◊ If you are going to be more free to facilitate learning and work with individuals or small groups, good behavior must be emphasized as essential. Praise is very necessary.

14. *Expect students to come to each lesson prepared.*

◊ Students need to accept the responsibility to report to class with the materials needed for each period. They will not have time to go to their "cubbies" to find what they need after a class is started.

◊ Coming to class prepared is part of the responsibility they need to take for themselves.

◊ Each student will need to bring at least a folder of some type with paper in it, if not a notebook, to each class period. Encourage carrying a notebook with a zipper pocket for pencils, erasers, scissors, rulers, pens, markers, etc., so that students won't be wasting time going back to "cubbies" to get these supplies that they will need for almost every class they report to.

15. Encourage students to get help from each other as needed.

◊ When your classroom is multi-age, and you want learners to take advantage of that fact, they need to be taught to get help from each other, when they can, instead of coming to you for every answer.

◊ Students also must be taught that it is their responsibility to help other classmates learn when needed. It is important that you see that your best students are not overburdened by requests for help, but many of them do have the time.

◊ The responsibility for seeing that others have the opportunity to learn needs to be shifted from you alone, to you and each of your students.

◊ Students who explain materials to others are gaining by doing so, as it helps them to clarify their thinking.

◊ Children need to understand why they are expected to work together and to help each other. That also includes understanding the necessity for good behavior so that students can learn in your classroom environment.

◊ If students stay on task, help each other, and don't interfere with the learning of others, then everyone will be much more likely to be successful.

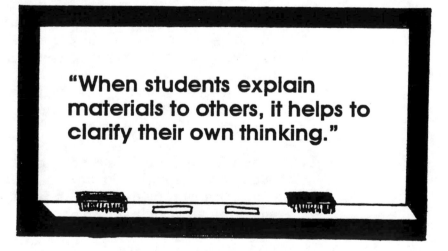

"When students explain materials to others, it helps to clarify their own thinking."

16. Post assignments and due dates so children will know when work must be completed.

◊ When students are working on many different projects and many of these are research-oriented, they will often be long term assignments.

◊ It is necessary to break long term assignments down into segments, with each expected to be done by a certain time. This helps students who tend to put things off and not keep up, so they don't go for a long period of time without completing anything, then find that they are not able to finish on time.

◊ Due dates should be posted on blackboards, and also included on assignment sheets that are given to students. When children are not all working on the same assignment, it is more difficult to keep track of when work should be completed.

◊ Different students could often have different due dates for current projects. Keeping due dates posted is also helpful for the child who needs to learn to keep track of these expectations but needs reminders.

17. Include expectations and due dates for projects in letters to parents.

◊ It is helpful to include expectations and due dates in notes to parents so they can also help their children accept responsibility for completing assignments.

◊ Parents appreciate knowing what their children are doing in school, and when they know, can help you to monitor progress.

◊ You should try to write a class newsletter, perhaps every Friday, or every other Friday, just to inform parents of what is happening in your classroom. This does not have to be long and can just be a short note. It helps if parents know when to expect to hear from you, so you should send notes at regular intervals. Students can also help you to write notes for home.

ADVICE FROM THE EXPERTS

"Use the circle discussion to help children become aware of their feelings, thoughts, and behaviors, to develop self-confidence, and to become interpersonally competent. Children need to learn that it is important to listen to develop awareness of the feelings of others. All children's comments need to be accepted as important. No put-downs are allowed."
Larry Chase
The Other Side of the Report Card

"Instead of seeing the teacher as the major resource, students in cooperative classrooms come to view their peers as important and valuable sources of knowledge."
Susan E. Ellis and Susan F. Whalen
Cooperative Learning: Getting Started

"Studying themes means the children must cooperate in order to learn and in so doing, they learn to cooperate."
Ruth Gamberg, Winniefred Kwak, Meredith Hutchings, and Judy Altheim
Learning and Loving It: Theme Studies in the Classroom

"Greater achievement is typically found in collaborative situations where peers work together than in situations where individuals work alone."
David W. Johnson and Roger T. Johnson
Learning Together and Alone

SCHEDULING:
A LOOK AT TYPICAL DAYS
IN THE CLASSROOM

MORNING MEETING

The day should begin with a morning meeting, where all of the children are called together. The purpose of the morning meeting is to discuss and make plans for the day. Children will look at the schedule that is posted, listen to announcements, and then fill out their schedules for the day. Daily activities will be planned according to the directions of the teacher and the choices of the students.

Attendance will be taken and children will share with the group if they have something they wish to show or tell. This is also a good time for the teacher to set a positive tone for the day by complimenting children on how well they did the day before, or letting them know that their attitudes and behavior are appreciated, that other adults are also proud of their performance, etc.

SCHEDULES

Each student should be given a weekly schedule at the beginning of the week. The schedule should include classes and activities for the week that are set for certain times and cannot be changed. It should also include times for children to make choices about what to do.

CHOICE PERIODS (See Schedule A--p. 70.)

Each day, the teacher should list good choices on the chalkboard or on a chart that can be posted, to remind children of work that can or should be completed. Choices should be discussed with students so they will choose wisely. Students will choose activities to do when they feel best about doing them, according to their interests, abilities, and learning styles.

NUMBERED PERIODS (See Schedule B--p. 71.)

When all students will be completing the same activities, but on a teacher directed rotation basis, the periods can be numbered and the children can be told what to do during each period of the day. One or more of these periods can still be student choice times, but at least one of the numbered periods will be spent with a certain activity required by the teacher. For management, it is a good idea to keep these periods the same during the week. Give each student a slip at the beginning of the week, indicating where they are to report for each of the numbered periods. They should immediately transfer the information on this slip to their daily schedule for the week.

COOPERATIVE GROUP OR DIRECT INSTRUCTION TIMES

If children are working together on activities, either in pairs or in small groups, they will need to make arrangements to schedule activities during the same time periods. If the teacher needs to call a small group together for instruction, children will need to fill in these group activities before they make choices for individual activities.

FULL GROUP ACTIVITIES

If the teacher needs to work with the entire group at the same time, this should be noted and discussed so children will fill in the correct time periods for meeting with the teacher before making indivdual choices.

INDEPENDENT ACTIVITIES

Students can be assigned to spend a certain period of time working independently, either alone, with a partner, or with a small group without teacher direction. This is usually a time when the teacher is involved in direct instruction and should not be bothered unless it is absolutely necessary. Peers can be chosen as leaders during this time period, so students can go to them if they need help with something. Discipline expectations should be well understood so that children will accomplish what they are meant to do during these periods.

END OF DAY MEETING

Students should be called back together at the end of each day to discuss the day's activities and to think ahead about plans for the following day. Positive thoughts about the day should be shared by the children and by the teacher. Reminders can be given for homework or assignments that need to be worked on at home, announcements can be made and flyers or papers that need to go home can be passed out. Students can also make note of anything they may need to bring from home for the next day.

DAILY SCHEDULE A

Time	Monday	Tuesday	Wednesday	Thursday	Friday
9:00	PLAN	PLAN	PLAN	PLAN	PLAN
9:20	**CHOICE**	**CHOICE** Orchestra 9:55	**CHOICE**	**CHOICE**	**CHOICE** Orchestra 9:55
10:35	RECESS	RECESS	RECESS	RECESS	RECESS
10:55	11:00 P.E. 11:30 MUSIC	11:00 P.E. 11:30 MUSIC	11:00 PE 11:30 MUSIC 11:25 Lunch Cart	LIBRARY	11:00 PE 11:30 MUSIC
12:00	READ ALOUD	READ ALOUD	READ ALOUD	READ ALOUD	READ ALOUD
12:20	LUNCH	LUNCH	LUNCH	LUNCH	LUNCH
12:50	RECESS	RECESS	RECESS	RECESS	RECESS
1:20	**CHOICE**	**CHOICE**	**CHOICE**	**CHOICE**	**CHOICE**
2:15	RECESS	RECESS	RECESS	RECESS	RECESS
2:45	**CHOICE**	**CHOICE** Band 2:50	**CHOICE**	**CHOICE**	**CHOICE** Band 2:50
3:15	PLAN	PLAN	PLAN	PLAN	PLAN
3:30	DISMISSAL	DISMISSAL	DISMISSAL	DISMISSAL	DISMISSAL

CHOICES

Choices can include assignments that students have already been given, such as work related to themes, science projects, social studies reports, math activities, story writing, spelling practice, literature packets, journals, silent reading, record keeping tasks, learning center activities, etc.

DAILY SCHEDULE B

Time	Monday	Tuesday	Wednesday	Thursday	Friday
9:00	PLAN	PLAN	PLAN	PLAN	PLAN
9:20	PERIOD ONE	PERIOD ONE Orchestra 9:55	PERIOD ONE	PERIOD ONE	PERIOD ONE Orchestra 9:55
10:15	OPTIONAL	OPTIONAL	OPTIONAL	OPTIONAL	OPTIONAL
10:30	RECESS	RECESS	RECESS	RECESS	RECESS
10:50	PERIOD TWO	PERIOD TWO	PERIOD TWO	PERIOD TWO	PERIOD TWO
11:35	READ ALOUD	READ ALOUD	READ ALOUD	READ ALOUD	READ ALOUD
12:00	LUNCH RECESS	LUNCH RECESS	LUNCH RECESS	Lunch Cart 12:00 LUNCH RECESS	LUNCH RECESS
1:00	PERIOD THREE	PERIOD THREE Band 1:20	PERIOD THREE Library Green 1:15	PERIOD THREE	PERIOD THREE Library-Blue 1:15
1:45	SCI. (1) S.S. (2)	SCI. (2) S.S. (1)	ART	SCI. (1) S.S. (2)	SCI. (2) S.S. (1)
2:15	RECESS	RECESS	RECESS	RECESS	RECESS
2:45	P.E. (B) MUSIC (A)	P.E. (A) MUSIC (B)	ART	P.E. (B) MUSIC (A) Band 2:50	P.E. (A) MUSIC (B)
3:15	PLAN	PLAN	PLAN	PLAN	PLAN
3:30	DISMISSAL	DISMISSAL	DISMISSAL	DISMISSAL	DISMISSAL

THREE PERIODS
Student or Teacher Choice--Reading, Math, and Independent Activities, such as direct teacher instruction, theme studies, silent reading, journals, literature packets, math computation, spelling activities, research projects, problem solving, learning center activities, record keeping, portfolio evaluations, adding to wall charts, etc.

GROUPING STRATEGIES

Ability Grouping--Not recommended
Dividing children into high, middle, and low groups.

Achievement Grouping
This is used for sequential lessons, as children move along a continuum of skills. Children of varying ages and abilities would be at the same achievement level, therefore achievement groups would usually contain children of mixed ages, with some students high, some average, and some lower in ability.

Interest Grouping
This is used when children have a choice to choose a certain type of project, giving them a chance to work with other children with the same interests.

Cooperative Grouping
This should be used when you purposely make up a group, with children as different, or as heterogeneous as possible. The group should contain children of all ages, with different abilities and learning styles. Members will learn from each other as they solve a problem or perform a task.

Learning Styles Grouping
This is used when children are given assignments that fit their learning styles, giving them optimum chances for success. Children with the same learning styles can work together on activities.

> Visual learners--need to watch and see. Give visual projects, using videos, pictures, charts, diagrams, verbal descriptions, etc.

> Auditory learners--need conversation and dialogue--can follow oral directions. Give auditory projects, with lectures, group discussions, auditory tapes etc.

> Tactile/kinesthetic learners--need action and movement, need to touch. Give hands-on activities, using manipulatives.

Random Grouping
This is used when likenesses and differences in children don't matter. It can be used to give the children a chance to sit and work with many different individuals, such as for home-room seating, art project time, lunch periods, game times, etc.

WORKING WITH
BLOOM'S TAXONOMY

Follow Bloom's Taxonomy of cognitive objectives and use the following descriptions and process verbs frequently with students. If they are taught the levels of thinking, they will understand how to increase their learning. Be sure that the inquiries you set up for children include verbs from the higher levels of the taxonomy. Have them answer and write questions from each of the levels as soon as they are capable of doing so.

Post the levels and the process verbs on bulletin boards, teach lessons on each level and often ask students to write questions for their classmates to answer, covering material you are studying.

Plan to have each student make a little book with one page for each level of thinking. Have them write the level at the top of the page and then list the process verbs that are on each level on the correct page. They will have this book to refer to as they are working.

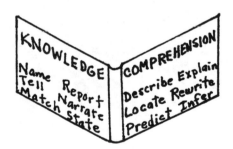

KNOWLEDGE:

Knowledge is defined as recalling or recognizing information, and/or remembering previously learned material. This is the lowest level of learning in the cognitive domain.

Process verbs to use are:

define, repeat, list, memorize, name, label, record, recall, relate, tell, report, narrate, state, select, match.

COMPREHENSION:

Comprehension is defined as having the ability to grasp the meaning of information. This may be changing material from one form to another or interpreting meaning. This is one step above remembering and the lowest level of understanding.

Process verbs to use are:

restate, describe, explain, identify, report, discuss, recognize, express, locate, review, estimate, generalize, extend, give examples, infer, paraphrase, summarize, predict, rewrite.

APPLICATION:

Application is defined as solving a problem using knowledge and appropriate generalizations. This is the ability to use learned material in new situations. This requires a higher level of understanding than the comprehension level.

Process verbs to use are:

demonstrate, practice, interview, apply, translate, dramatize, operate, schedule, illustrate, interpret, change, compute, discover, solve, manipulate, modify.

ANALYSIS:

Analysis is described as separating information into component parts so you can understand its organizational structure. This is a higher level than comprehension and application because it requires an understanding of both the content and the structure of material.

Process verbs to use are:

debate, distinguish, question, differentiate, solve, diagram, compare, inventory, criticize, experiment, discriminate, illustrate, outline.

SYNTHESIS:

Synthesis is described as solving a problem by putting together information that requires original, creative thinking. This is the ability to put parts together to form a new whole, encouraging creative behaviors.

Process verbs to use are:

compose, propose, formulate, assemble, construct, design, arrange, organize, prepare, classify, plan, compile, categorize, devise, reconstruct, reorganize, revise, rewrite, rearrange.

EVALUATION:

Evaluation is described as making qualitative and quantitative judgments according to set standards. It involves the ability to judge the value of material, based on definite criteria. Learning outcomes here are the highest level, as all of the other levels are involved.

Process verbs to use are:

select, judge, predict, choose, estimate, measure, value, rate, assess, appraise, compare, conclude, contrast, discriminate, justify, interpret, support, explain.

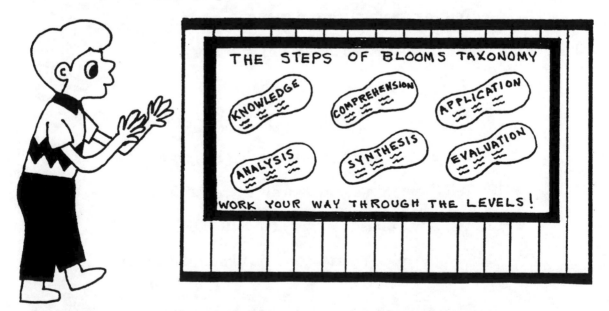

Adapted from the list by Benjamin S. Bloom, in <u>Bloom's Taxonomy of Educational Objectives: Cognitive Domain</u>. New York: David McKay, 1956.

QUESTIONING STRATEGIES WITH BLOOM'S TAXONOMY

TYPICAL INQUIRIES ON EACH LEVEL

When planning thematic units be sure to include inquiries on the different levels of Bloom's Taxonomy. Build your units around inquiries such as the following:

<u>KNOWLEDGE LEVEL</u>--to know or to recall an answer.

1. Name a conflict that your character/characters had.

2. List the events that happened.

3. Tell which animals were in this story.

4. Tell five things that happened.

5. Explain the who, what, when, and where.

6. State what happened in chronological order.

7. Tell the seven historical events.

8. Name the main character in your story.

9. Name the hero in the first chapter.

10. Tell about the problem the main character had.

11. Write three questions about what happened.

12. Tell three things you read about the setting.

13. Tell five things that Betty forgot to tell Sue about.

14. List the main characters and tell how the author described each one.

15. Give examples of the food that the Pilgrims ate.

16. Describe the shelters used by the pioneers.

COMPREHENSION LEVEL--to explain or understand an answer.

1. Explain how the challenge, the character had, changed his life.

2. Describe the solutions to the characters' conflicts.

3. Describe how the character felt when his dog died.

4. Describe the lesson learned in this fable.

5. Explain why you would say the character in this story was selfish.

6. Explain why you think Sue and Joe would make good friends.

7. Write a summary of what happened.

8. Describe an event that made you laugh.

9. Write a paragraph about an interesting event.

10. Describe the main events in sequential order.

11. Describe the setting well enough for us to picture it.

12. Explain the plot of this story.

13. Describe the region of the world where this story takes place.

14. Tell how the characters resolved the conflicts.

15. Write a summary of what happened to your character.

16. Outline the steps Amanda used to write her paper.

17. Explain why laws are necessary in America.

18. Interpret the chart on water temperatures on page 15.

19. Give reasons for the Revolutionary War.

20. Demonstrate your understanding of Phillip's problems.

APPLICATION LEVEL--to use knowledge and ideas to solve problems.

1. Draw a picture showing how the puppy felt when his master left.

2. Collect examples of pictures to fit the setting in your story.

3. Identify five things in your bedroom at home that would not have been in Samantha's room.

4. Construct a bench out of toothpicks to put in your pioneer display.

5. Pretend that you are in the place of the character. Write a diary about a day in your life.

6. Write a newspaper article that could help you find the lost dog in your story.

7. Find examples in the story which tell you what kind of person Sarah was.

8. Write a newspaper ad that Mafu might have written to convince people to go on his voyage.

9. Describe the plot of the story in sequence.

10. Make a poster to use in persuading a friend to read the book.

11. Write a "Dear Abby" letter to explain Sammy's problems.

12. Change the title of each chapter in the book to your own words.

13. Write an interview that Mr. Barnes may have given to Miss Smith.

14. Schedule a day of activities that would make your day similar to Bob's.

15. Research the country in the story, then make a travel brochure to advertise the country to a traveler.

16. Give an example of another setting where this story could have taken place.

ANALYSIS LEVEL--to break down or take apart information.

1. Separate the story events into good and evil happenings.

2. Simplify the dance steps shown so you can teach them to a friend.

3. Outline the important events that took place.

4. Compare John's job to Robert's job.

5. Examine the story for reasons Patricia was so mad.

6. Explain what parts of the story helped to set the scary mood.

7. Write a debate that might have taken place between Mr. Barnes and Roughby Miller.

8. Explain the situations that made this a humorous story.

9. Construct a "How-to" chart from the story you read about construction of model airplanes.

10. Distinguish between yourself and the main character in this story when it comes to feelings toward school.

11. Write a criticism of the way Mr. Smithby treated Anna.

12. Explain how Mrs. Johnston handled being handicapped.

13. Explain what happened in this story that could not have really happened.

14. Differentiate between the two sisters when it came to going to church.

15. Outline the stages Samantha went through as she tried to deal with the loss of her father.

16. Criticize the way Joseph played in the baseball game after he lost his temper.

17. Compare and contrast the characters' feelings at the beginning and at the end of the story.

18. List the events that led to solving the mystery in sequential order.

SYNTHESIS LEVEL--to form a new whole by putting information together.

1. Find an unusual way to report on what you read about wildflowers.

2. Develop a plan for your classroom to make money for a field trip.

3. Create a model of a game that explains the story you just read.

4. Produce an object that could help you with your homework.

5. Create an invention that would make your life easier.

6. Compose a song that Sally might have sung to her father.

7. Make up a play to tell the story of Mary's life in France.

8. Generate an idea that would convince your parents to give you a higher allowance like the one Jerry had.

9. State the reasons why you think that science experiment will work.

10. Imagine someone you know and write a story that would turn him/her into a hero or heroine.

11. Write another short episode for this adventure story.

12. Choose an event that happened in your book and change it so that it would have changed the course of history.

13. Write a new ending for this story.

14. Prepare a dialogue that could have taken place between you and the main character in the story.

15. Write a brief speech you would give if you were expected to introduce Mr. Carlson to your football team.

16. Pretend you are a talk show host and write a set of questions you would like to ask your favorite character.

17. Write yourself into a fantasy story and explain the role you would like to play.

EVALUATION LEVEL--to justify actions or judge events.

1. Explain why you would or would not pay higher taxes as Jeremy was told to do in the story.

2. Write a note to the author of the book telling why you did or did not like the book.

3. Categorize your favorite characters from Dr. Seuss books, explaining how each of them make you feel.

4. Evaluate the high salaries athletes make and explain why you think this is right or wrong.

5. Criticize the statement that Jerry made to Martha.

6. Justify why you would recommend a book to a friend.

7. Judge the value of the painting on the museum wall.

8. List the exaggerations used in the story and explain which ones were helpful to the plot.

9. Give three reasons why you think the French Revolution happened.

10. Support why you think it was beneficial to read this article.

11. Describe the importance that computers will have in your life.

12. Read two different accounts of the same historical event. Tell which one seems to be the most realistic.

13. Justify your reasons for not wanting to vote for a Presidential candidate.

14. Defend the actions of the boys against the girls in the contest.

15. Conclude the action you think should be taken against the criminals.

16. Write a newspaper or television review to rate the book you read.

17. Evaluate the mystery you read for suspense, alibis, and clues.

PROJECTS FOR ACTIVE LEARNERS

These activities are designed to be motivating and to give children a great variety of choices as to how they can demonstrate their understanding of material they have covered. Add information from your current topics to each project to make it fit your curriculum. Projects of this type are especially valuable as children will most likely go beyond the knowledge and comprehension level in order to complete them.

An active classroom is a special place to be, and a great deal of learning will go on if you use projects such as the following when planning your thematic units. When you are ready to plan a unit, look through the list to see which activities could be built into the unit you are putting together. Students can also look at the list and decide which activities they would be interested in doing as part of your unit.

1. Create a diorama showing the setting and/or characters.

2. Sculpt scenes and characters out of clay, toothpicks, cotton, felt, cloth, etc.

3. Watch a film and take notes on what you see and hear.

4. Plan a debate between two individuals.

5. Write a letter to a character.

6. Make up a newspaper ad fitting the story.

7. Write a letter to an author.

8. Create a comic strip.

9. Dress up like characters.

10. Design a game.

11. Create a movie.

12. Write an essay.

13. Draw a picture.

14. Illustrate a story.

15. Draw a set of pictures, in strip form.

16. Design a lesson on the computer.

17. Be a talk-show host.

18. Design a bulletin board.

19. Make a chart showing sequence of events.

20. Make a graph.

21. Label a drawing or diagram.

22. Do a choral reading with a partner or group.

23. Construct a display.

24. Interview a character or a famous person.

25. Write a song and perform it for an audience.

26. Draw a map with a scale or legend.

27. Make a collage.

28. Write a letter to an editor.

29. Collect articles to share.

30. Give a demonstration.

31. Make a crossword puzzle.

32. Do an experiment.

33. Make a large-scale drawing.

34. Create a mobile.

35. Construct a model.

36. Write a radio program.

37. Listen to or make an audio tape.

38. Watch or create a video tape.

39. Write a newspaper story.

40. Make transparencies to show.

41. Write a petition.

42. Design a poster.

43. Make up a play.

44. Take a survey.

45. Paint a picture.

46. Construct a pamphlet or brochure.

47. Design and construct a puppet.

48. Put on a puppet play.

49. Design and paint a mural.

50. Give an oral report.

51. Build with papier mache.

52. Make up riddles or limericks.

53. Give a slide show.

54. Hold a press conference.

55. Put on a skit.

MANAGEMENT USING NOVELS FOR LITERATURE INSTRUCTION

ROTATION METHOD

Divide the class into four groups according to instructional reading levels. Assign novels or give the groups several novels to choose from, but all members of the same group must work on the same book. For the first couple of days, give everyone time to read in their novels. You may wish to have students start a journal and write a little about the story each day, after they read.

Starting on about the third day, after everyone has had time to read part of the book, set up a rotation schedule. Designate four areas in the room for student groups to rotate to during rotation periods. Give each group a name, such as the title of the book, colors, numbers, etc. Give each group cards telling them which rotation to start with, and what order to follow, or post a chart for them to look at when necessary.

Have students spend about 30 minutes in their first rotation, and then quickly and quietly move to the second one. The third and fourth rotation would usually be made on the next day. Continue this rotation until groups have completed their novels.

Rotation One--read the novel, and keep track of the pages completed.

Rotation Two--write in a journal or complete an assigned activity related to the book. These may be skills lessons, worksheets, writing assignments, etc. but the lesson should be related to the novel being read. Creative expression activities, such as drama, would also fit here.

Rotation Three--meet with the teacher to discuss the book and the assignments.

NOTE: For rotations two and three, be sure to cover only the parts of the book that have been read by the slowest reader in the group. The slowest readers should be encouraged to find extra time to read, however, either during the school day or at home, so they have a chance to catch up with the faster readers in their groups.

Rotation Four--work at a learning center, or complete skills lessons that are needed. These may be lessons needed in reading, spelling, or writing skills, and do not necessarily have to be related to the novel.

85

WORKING WITH INDIVIDUAL NOVEL GROUPS

Divide the class into groups of four or five, according to instructional reading levels. Give each group several novels to choose from that correspond with the correct reading level so the group can decide which book to read. All students in each group will need to read the same book.

Have students read the books, write in journals, do daily skills assignments, discuss what they are reading and work on assignments together as they read. Expect each child to keep a record of what has been read and what assignments have been completed that are related to the book.

When all of the members of a group have finished the book, have them do a final presentation together to share the book with the rest of the class.

Meet with each group every second or third day long enough to see where they are, check comprehension, give assignments, evaluate what they have completed, etc. This does not have to be a formal meeting, but may just be sitting down with a group and participating in whatever they are working on at the moment.

USING INTEREST GROUPS OR THEMATIC INSTRUCTION

There are times when individual students or small groups of students will want to read books according to interest or following the theme that the class is currently working on without regard to ability levels. In this case you may want to have all students read silently at the same time and then have individuals and groups work on activities at the same time.

This method gives students a silent room for reading, followed by an active time where students share with each other and learn from what each student is reading and working on at the time. Celebrations and sharing of material should follow as books are finished and projects are completed.

AUTHOR'S NOTE: SEE MY BOOK, CREATIVE PROJECTS FOR INDEPENDENT LEARNERS, CATS PUBLICATIONS, 1995, FOR A DETAILED ACCOUNT OF USING NOVELS FOR READING INSTRUCTION. PROJECTS AND IDEAS INCLUDED HELP STUDENTS WITH COMPREHENSION AND HIGHER-LEVEL THINKING SKILLS AND ARE DESIGNED TO FIT ANY NOVEL.

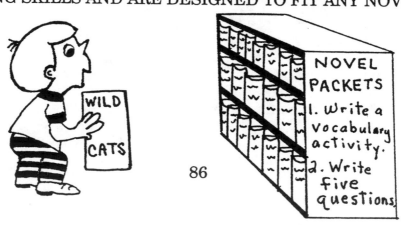

86

HELPING CHILDREN TO DISCOVER THEMSELVES AND OTHERS

Children need to use their imaginations and talk and write about their own feelings and the feelings of others. They will develop closer relationships with others when they talk and write about each other.

◊ They need opportunities to let others know what they are thinking and feeling.

◊ They need to be aware of other people's feelings and describe how they would act if they were in the same position.

◊ They need to know that many other children have the same feelings, fears, concerns, likes, dislikes, interests, etc., that they have.

◊ They need to understand that many other children feel differently than they do.

◊ They need to develop empathy for the way other people feel and act.

◊ They need to think about how they affect other people and how other people affect them.

◊ They need to look at their world and at themselves from the eyes of another person at times.

◊ They need to express themselves and listen to others express themselves, both creatively and critically.

◊ They need to know that it is okay to express a different opinion and learn to respect the opinions of others.

Children need to imagine what they would do if their world were suddenly different. They are more likely to appreciate what they have now, if they think about what would happen should they suddenly not have everything they are used to having.

◊ They need to fantasize about what they would do if certain impossible dreams came true.

◊ They should be aware of objects and belongings around them, and think about what would happen if these things were suddenly different or gone.

◊ They should think of the consequences if they had everything they wanted and didn't need anything more.

◊ They need to talk about how a different world would affect their family.

Ask students to consider and express themselves on questions such as the following:

ALL ABOUT YOU

1. How would you feel if you were 6 feet tall?

2. How would you feel if you weighed 300 pounds?

3. How would you feel if you were 3 years old?

4. How would you feel if you were President John F. Kennedy?

5. How would you feel if you were an astronaut?

6. What would you see, hear, taste, and smell if you were at a carnival?

7. What would you see, hear, and smell if you were in a lightning storm?

ALL ABOUT YOU AND OTHERS

1. If you were your father, how would he feel about giving you an allowance?

2. If you were your mother, what would be the first thing she'd think when she opened your bedroom door after you've left for school?

3. What would your cat think about your bringing home a new puppy?

4. How would your older sister feel if you wore her favorite outfit?

5. How would your grandmother feel if you called her on the telephone?

6. How would your new kitten feel if you forgot to feed it?

7. What would your sister think if you bought her a special present?

8. Which person do you feel has had the most influence on your life?

9. How many ways would you be able to help your mother at home?

10. How many words can you think of that would describe your best friend?

11. If you could change one personality trait of your brother's, what would it be?

12. If you could have one personality trait of your brother's, what would it be?

IF ONLY YOU COULD

1. If you could have $100 to spend, what would you buy?

2. If you could be another person who is living today, who would it be?

3. If you could be a famous person from the past, who would it be?

4. If you could have anything you wanted to eat for dinner tonight, what would it be?

5. If you could go to any movie this weekend, what would you see?

6. If you could be on a television show, which one would you like to star in?

IF YOUR WORLD SHOULD CHANGE

1. What would happen if you suddenly had no home to go to?

2. What would happen if an earthquake hit your town?

3. What would happen if your dog bit you tonight?

4. What if 4 feet of snow fell tonight? How would it affect you and your family?

5. What if there wasn't any money left in the world? What would we do to get what we need?

6. How would you feel if there were no television?

7. How would you feel if there were no music or art in the world?

8. What would happen if all of your toys were suddenly burned?

9. What would you do if you couldn't take part in any sports?

10. What if you couldn't go to school anymore? How would it make you feel?

THROUGH THE EYES OF OTHERS

1. How would a blind person feel in a thunder storm?

2. What does an elephant look like to a small child?

3. How would the ugly witch have told the story of Hansel and Gretel?

4. What would it be like to be a lonely little old lady?

IF IT COULD BE REAL

1. What would it feel like to be an electric frying pan?

2. How would you feel if you were a Christmas tree?

3. What would it feel like to fly above your house?

4. What would happen if up was down and down was up?

5. What would happen if there were no weekends?

6. Suppose you could go back in time. How far back would you go?
   What would you be?

AN OVERVIEW OF MATHEMATICS REFORM

According to the National Council of Teachers of Mathematics, as stated in their 1989 document, *Curriculum and Evaluation Standards for School Mathematics,* problem solving needs to be the way of the future as far as teaching mathematics is concerned. This is their recommendation for mathematics reform, in order to prepare students to compete and work in a highly technological society.

The document consists of a broad framework to guide reform in mathematics curriculum, in terms of content priority and emphasis. Mathematics consists of a number of different strands, and each strand is deserving of attention. According to the document, math instruction in the past has consisted mainly of individual practice with number operations and computation, while the other strands of mathematics have received a very small percentage of time in most classrooms. It is stated that there is a need for change in the way mathematics is taught and these changes are summarized.

Many states and school districts have used this document as a guide and have designed their mathematics programs to include more emphasis on all of the strands of mathematics. The separate strands have been identified with different titles, and grouped differently by many educators, but each strand is included in most cases.

THE NEED FOR A CHANGE

Technological advances in our society require that children be prepared differently in mathematics, as the work force must depend on highly literate employees who can think for themselves and make informed decisions about mathematical situations. There is a need for excellence in mathematical concepts, and the ability to apply what is known to real life situations. The memorization of rules and procedures that has been the way of math in the past, will not prepare students for the high expectations of employers. Students will need meaningful experiences with the operations of mathematics in order to see and understand the relationships that exist, and apply this information to their daily lives.

Working with hands-on manipulative objects is essential in order to develop concepts so that children will see the meaning behind mathematics. They need to construct their own understanding with concrete objects, before they are expected to manipulate symbols, as the symbols have no meaning of their own, except for the meaning that the student brings to the situation.

In many classrooms, students have been spending too much time working with abstract symbols, attempting to determine answers to computational problems, without any understanding of why numbers work as they do. There is now a push for small group problem solving activities in all of the strands of mathematics, so that children can work together while pursuing problems directly related to real life experiences. These activities will help children to develop mathematical concepts before they are expected to work with abstract symbols.

Paper and pencil activities have been the major component of math instruction in the past. It is now recommended that a great deal of time needs to be spent working individually and in groups on mental computation, estimation, and problem solving. Students will also need to become proficient with the use of a calculator. Computational skills are still very important and need emphasis, but the other strands of mathematics can no longer be considered as just supplementary topics. Computational skills can and should be used while working on all of the strands, and should be integrated into problem solving situations.

THE RATIONALE FOR STRESSING PROBLEM SOLVING

◊ Reasoning skills need to be developed in order for students to become productive citizens.

◊ Concrete experiences in real life situations must be used for developing math concepts, as children must have an understanding of concepts before they work with abstract symbols, if math is to have any meaning to them.

◊ Relationships among concepts from the different strands and the patterns of mathematics need to be discovered in manipulative situations with concrete objects.

◊ Student understanding of the reasonableness of answers needs to be developed through estimation activities.

◊ Students need to learn different strategies for solving problems, such as looking for patterns, drawing diagrams, guessing and checking, constructing tables or graphs, building models, making lists, acting out situations, etc.

◊ Thinking is clarified through participation in group activities where children communicate understanding of mathematical concepts through discussions, writing in journals or learning logs, drawings, displays, etc.

A LOOK AT MATHEMATICS IN AN INTEGRATED PROGRAM

A Period of Its Own

Mathematics will sometimes need to be considered as a separate subject. It is important to be sure that enough time is being devoted to mathematics, according to the potential and achievement of individual students. If math is always tied to thematic instruction units, it is likely that students will not have enough practice on their own achievement levels to learn the necessary concepts and skills for each mathematical strand.

> **"While some aspects of mathematics should be integrated through themes and topics of study, it is appropriate to introduce and practice some mathematical concepts and skills in specific blocks of instructional time devoted to mathematics."**
> **British Columbia,** *Primary Program*

Problem Solving

Problem solving activities need to be built into all strands of mathematics. If these activities can be planned around your classroom theme, they will be especially meaningful. Experiences of this type should be built into your curriculum whenever possible, but it is difficult to design problems fitting all of the strands, while also fitting your classroom theme. Extra problem solving activities will most likely need to be designed around strands to be covered that do not fit into your thematic units. These can be completed during separate math periods.

With the wide range of ability in a multi-age classroom, it is also difficult to design problems, fitting a theme, that children can all work on at the same time without the problems being too easy for some and too hard for others. It usually is an advantage for the younger or lower students to work with the older or higher students and be exposed to material on many different skill levels. Each student will gain what he/she is ready for from these experiences. However, all students need to be spending some time solving problems on their own skill levels in order to develop needed concepts.

A LOOK AT MATHEMATICS IN A MULTI-AGE CLASSROOM

Problem solving activities for math are especially beneficial to students in a multi-age classroom. Due to the nature of the classroom, with the stress on cooperative group activities and peer tutoring, this type of math instruction follows the multi-age philosophy of teaching and learning, where students gain from the experiences of others.

The Benefits for Multi-age Students

◊ Problem solving activities are deliberately designed containing multiple levels of learning.

◊ Students will learn what they can from their first exposure to material by listening to and working with students on higher levels.

◊ Concepts need to be repeated through the years so that the knowledge gained is reinforced and expanded each time a student is exposed to it.

◊ Previously learned concepts and skills will continue to be reinforced regularly in a multi-age setting.

◊ Students will learn to apply their skills as they discuss their understandings, listen to the interpretations of other students, and write about what they have learned.

◊ Some activities will be designed for independent learning at first, so students can try on their own, but then they will have the benefit of discussing their findings with others.

◊ Students who are slower to understand abstract concepts will have the help of more able students.

◊ Following assessment, small groups or individuals can be retaught concepts and students who understand can help with the reteaching.

◊ Experiences with mental math and estimation on different skill levels will be especially helpful to the younger student.

MATH STRATEGIES FOR INDIVIDUALIZED OR SMALL GROUP INSTRUCTION

FOLLOW STUDENT LEARNING OBJECTIVES

◊ Divide your math instruction program into the different strands, such as numbers and operations, measurement, geometry, and statistics and probability.

◊ Make a list of the objectives for each strand. In strands where there is a sequence, such as in numbers and operations, place these objectives along a continuum. If sequence doesn't matter, just list them in a logical order.

◊ Compare the objectives of different grade levels, and include those above and below the levels you are teaching.

◊ Introduce each strand early in the year through problem solving activities. Have students write to explain what they have done in order to assess their understanding of concepts. Save these and use them to judge growth throughout the year.

"Compare the objectives of different grade levels, and include those above and below the levels you are teaching."

DECIDE ON ACTIVITIES

◊ Choose one strand to concentrate on at a given time, but when possible, integrate activities from different strands into your units.

◊ Locate group activities, by looking in books from at least two or three grade levels, finding books with problem solving activities, and/or use educational magazines with math ideas until you have enough problems on multiple levels for each objective.

◊ Integrate the other subjects into your math curriculum by planning math activities that fit your classroom theme.

◊ Create menus of hands-on problem solving activities to help students develop math concepts and thinking processes.

◊ Provide group activities that can be understood on many different levels, so the experiences will be beneficial to all students as they learn from each other.

◊ Provide time for individual assignments or independent work following the needs and interests of students.

◊ Plan some activities that call for estimation of answers, where an exact answer is not necessary.

◊ Set aside special time for needed practice on the mathematical operations of addition, subtraction, multiplication, division, fractions, and decimals.

◊ Provide some drill and practice on operations through games and puzzles.

◊ Build mental computation activities into your schedule each day.

◊ Promote the use of calculators, at times, when they are an efficient way to compute answers.

GUIDE STUDENTS THROUGH GROUP ACTIVITIES

◊ Encourage peer tutoring as students are working in their groups, so all children will understand the activity.

◊ Ask students questions such as the following:

Do you agree with Jim's answer?
Who has a different answer?
Can you explain how you got that solution?
Can you prove you are right?
Would that always be true?
Is your answer reasonable?
How does that compare to the last problem you did?

◊ Ask students to explain orally and in writing, what their answers are and how they obtained them.

DESIGN PERFORMANCE ASSESSMENTS FOR OBJECTIVES

◊ Build performance assessments into your program after each menu, to help guide further instruction.

◊ Design a rubric to be used to check for understanding.

◊ Include at least three response levels in rubrics.

> <u>High level response</u>--the child is able to show a transition from the use of manipulative objects to the working with abstract symbols and/or ideas, by completing and explaining the problem correctly.

> <u>Medium level response</u>--the child can complete and explain part of the problem correctly, but part of the problem is incorrect, or the explanation is inappropriate. Rules may not be clear or procedures may not be understood.

> <u>Low level response</u>--the child can complete part of the problem correctly, but there appears to be no understanding of concepts or relationships.

◊ Have individuals work alone on these assessments to show their understanding of concepts, before they begin the next activity.

◊ Assign review menus, when applicable, for those who don't understand the concepts the first time.

◊ Keep grouping flexible, as students are motivated by working with a variety of individuals and will gain different insights when working with different partners.

TEACHING THE SKILLS OF PROBLEM SOLVING

A major part of mathematics instruction needs to involve children working in groups with problem solving activities, while covering all of the strands. The skills of problem solving need to be taught and used by students as they investigate and experiment with hands-on materials to learn mathematical concepts. Only after they have this understanding of concepts can they work with the abstract equations and symbols of mathematics, if their work is to have any meaning to them.

Ways to Solve Problems

◊ Recognize that there is a problem to solve.

◊ Investigate the situation and clarify the problem, determining whether or not you have been given all of the needed information, then ask for what is missing, if necessary.

◊ Talk about it, look for key words, listen to each other's interpretations or other points of view, ask each other questions, and make connections to prior knowledge.

◊ Try different problem solving strategies, such as: act out the problem, break the problem into subtopics, guess and check, look for patterns, construct models, make drawings or charts, use manipulatives, construct graphs, draw diagrams, make lists or tables, use trial and error, classify or order information, etc.

◊ Use manipulatives, when possible, to solve problems or to show the validity of answers.

◊ Estimate answers or predict results, then determine the reasonableness of possible solutions.

◊ Write and solve number sentences when they are appropriate.

◊ Reflect on answers by talking about them, explaining your thinking to others, justifying your thinking, or writing about solutions and how they were found.

◊ Make visual displays to show solutions and to represent your interpretations of problems.

Sample Problem Solving Activities Following Strands

Strand--Numbers and Operations
Includes numeration, whole number concepts and operations, computation of whole numbers, functions, number relationships and patterns, estimation, number theory, fractions, and decimals.

1. Build strategies for solving number facts such as:
   Addition--using sums of 10, one more than, and doubles.
   Subtraction--one less than, opposite of addition, and counting backwards.
   Multiplication--building arrays, repeated addition, skip counting, and using times tables to see patterns.
   Division--separating arrays, repeated subtraction, and opposite of multiplication.

2. Build concepts of multiplication and division by combining and separating groups of objects.

3. Manipulate objects and groups of objects to show parts of a whole or parts of a group when learning fractions.

4. Fill in squares of a grid to show percentages or fractions.

5. Show place value with counters placed in groups of hundreds, tens, and ones.

Strand--Geometry
Includes shapes and dimensions of plane figures and three dimensional figures, symmetry, congruence, ordering on number grids, and using scale.

1. Learn to recognize examples of geometric figures such as circles, squares, triangles, rectangles, polygons, cones, cubes, spheres, pyramids, and cylinders by using manipulative objects.

2. Measure the diameters and circumferences of several round figures and determine the relationships between them.

3. Make a scale drawing of a favorite cartoon character by drawing a grid over the cartoon, then copying what you see on a larger scale.

4. Paste a geometric shape with a pattern in the middle of a piece of paper, then extend the pattern in all directions.

5. Draw objects as you would see them from different views.

Strand--Measurement
Includes length and capacity, area and perimeter, time, money, and temperature.

1. Use different units to measure the length of objects, then determine which is the most accurate.

2. Estimate, then order a set of objects by weight or volume.

3. Build a scale model of a building, or complete a scale drawing of your classroom.

4. Compare several objects with the same area, then measure the perimeters to determine relationships.

5. Experiment with ice cubes in water, using both Celsius and Fahrenheit thermometers, to help determine approximately what the freezing point of water and melting point of ice would be on the two temperature scales.

Strand--Statistics and Probablility
Includes data analysis, estimation, prediction, inference, and activities with chance.

1. Construct or interpret bar graphs, line graphs, circle graphs, pictographs, tally marks, diagrams, etc.

2. Take a survey and graph the results.

3. Use several spinners with sections marked off in different ways. Predict how many times the needle will stop in certain sections.

4. Collect data from random samples of a population, then from the total population. Determine how accurate your random sampling was in relation to the total population.

5. Determine the mean, the median, the mode, and the range from a set of numerical data collected as part of an experiment.

MATH MANAGEMENT
FOR COMPUTATION SKILLS

Computation skills continue to be important and must still be developed so that children can perform the operations of addition, subtraction, multiplication, division, fractions, and decimals, when necessary. The change in emphasis is that instead of just paper and pencil practice with algorithms, with no context, children should be introduced to these operations through problem solving activities with concrete objects. They need to develop concepts and gain an understanding of the processes before they work with the abstract symbols.

IMPORTANT CONSIDERATIONS

1. Calculators can and need to be used during problem solving activities, when it is an efficient and effective way to find answers, but they can not entirely take the place of learning computational skills.

2. Menus stressing the operations need to be an integral part of your math program, with problems designed on multiple levels.

3. Teaching for understanding is essential so that children can apply computational skills to real life situations.

4. Mental computation activities should be a regular part of your daily schedule.

5. Games and puzzles involving computation should be available on a regular basis.

6. Drill and practice should be used to develop number sense and to discover the relationships between operations.

7. Students must learn the basic facts in order to make estimations, or to perform calculations, either mentally or on paper. Facts need to be introduced through real life situations, but some children will need extra practice in order to master them.

8. Computation skills need to be assessed. You should know children's achievement levels on paper and pencil computation, mental computation, and estimation activities. Some children may benefit from extra practice on algorithms once they understand the processes.

AUTHENTIC ASSESSMENT AND EVALUATION

ASSESSMENT:

To observe and collect evidence to show what a child is capable of doing.

EVALUATION:

To study and interpret this evidence in order to make sound judgments and decisions about a child's progress.

PURPOSES OF ASSESSMENT AND EVALUATION:

To guide teachers as they make decisions about instructional programs.

To determine the strengths and weaknesses of each individual.

To make decisions about what specific instruction is needed by each individual.

To provide students and parents with information about a student's progress.

To support and verify the reporting of individual progress to parents.

To give direction to students and teachers as they set goals for future learning.

EVALUATION SHOULD BE BASED ON CLASSROOM OBSERVATIONS AND WORK COLLECTED FOR A PORTFOLIO.

A portfolio is a purposeful collection of student work. It is used to exhibit to the student, the teacher, and the parents the effort, progress, or achievement of the student. It is essential that the student participate in collecting material for the portfolio. The student should also reflect on the work chosen and include a written evaluation of the material, using the learner characteristics as a basis for judgment.

EVALUATION SHOULD INCLUDE INTERPRETATION OF:

Contents of portfolios

Anecdotal comments

Self-assessment

Photographs

Classroom tests

School and district exams

State exams

Standardized tests

Interviews and conferences with students and parents.

Interest inventories

Reading logs

Learning logs

Work samples

Audio tapes

Video tapes

Adapted from Robert Anthony, Terry Johnson, Norma I. Mickelson, and Alison Preece, University of Victoria, British Columbia. (See Reference Section)

EVALUATION AND ASSESSMENT

WITH LEARNER CHARACTERISTICS

> The following learner characteristics are to be used for evaluating students. Explain the definitions of these words to parents and use them for evaluating student work. Students should also be thinking in these terms and evaluating themselves and their classmates with them.

1. KNOWLEDGEABLE

This is having information stored in the brain which will help with making sense out of life experiences.

2. SELF-CONFIDENT

This is is the value a person places on his/her self image; what a person thinks about her/himself.

3. GENERATIVE

This involves being creative and coming up with new ideas but also producing new solutions to problems or responding differently by restating ideas developed by others.

4. RISK-TAKING

This is a willingness to try new ventures. It involves educated reasons for actions and is not just recklessness. Learning involves moving into new territory, territory that is unknown or unfamiliar.

5. THOUGHTFUL

This involves curiosity, reflection, insight, and critical judgment. Curiosity is a need to know and a willingness to find out. Reflection involves thinking things over. Insight involves understanding of why things are so. Critical judgment is applying known criteria to a situation to make a decision.

6. <u>RESOURCEFUL</u>

This is the capacity to bring personal experiences and resources to bear on a problem. Gathering and using these resources effectively is our goal.

7. <u>ORGANIZED</u>

This involves putting resources to work in such a way as to achieve a solution to a problem. This also includes keeping track of requirements and materials needed to solve a problem.

8. <u>COLLABORATIVE</u>

This is being able to work with others to achieve personal goals, but in a way that is also helpful to others. This is also being able to assist in achieving collective goals, and being sensitive to the feelings of other members of the group.

9. <u>INDUSTRIOUS</u>

This is being hardworking, and persistent even in the face of failure, trying again and seeing a job through to its completion.

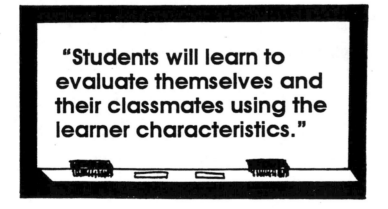

"Students will learn to evaluate themselves and their classmates using the learner characteristics."

Adapted from Robert Anthony, Terry Johnson, Norma I. Mickelson, and Alison Preece, University of Victoria, British Columbia. (See Reference Section)

LEARNING LOGS

Learning logs are another tool which should be used as a means of having children reflect on their own learning. Ask them often to answer a question where they will be evaluating their own performances. Stress self-evaluation of student work and behavior. Have students write in a spiral notebook or put together a small book to write in, as these pages should be saved.

The following is a writing frame for learning logs, which will help children to evaluate themselves and their classmates, using the learner characteristics.

I WAS _____ TODAY WHEN I _____ .

TOMORROW, I WILL TRY TO BE MORE _____ .

I NOTICED _____ WAS _____

TODAY WHEN _____ .

Children should take time to write in their learning logs several times a week. It helps them to think about themselves and others, and to see how well they are exhibiting the learner characteristics that you are evaluating.

Ask students to explain in their learning logs what a certain characteristic means to them and how well they are doing with it. They can also write what they intend to do in order to improve.

ORGANIZED
1. What does organized mean?
2. Are you organized?
3. What can you do to improve your organization in school and at home?

NOTE: Credit for the learning log frame is given to Kathryn Turnbull of John Muir Elementary School, Sooke, B.C. She was a student of Robert Anthony's at the University of Victoria. (See References.)

LEARNING LOGS WRITTEN BY CHILDREN

My Learning Log   Barbara
  I was thoughtful today when I worked with my science experiment. I was curious to find out what would happen if I stirred food coloring into hot water instead of cold, so I tried it. It moved faster in hot water.
  Tomorrow I will try to be more organized because I couldn't find my math paper this morning.

My Learning Log   Jim
  I was industrious today when I finished two pages in my math book. Tomorrow I will try to be more collaborative when I work with my science group and let everyone have a chance to use the materials.

MY LEARNING LOG   BETTY
I NOTICED AMANDA WAS GENERATIVE TODAY WHEN SHE TRIED ALL OF THE COLORS MIXED TOGETHER IN ART TO SEE WHAT COLOR THEY WOULD MAKE. IT WAS UGLY SO SHE LEFT OUT THE BLACK AND THE BROWN THE SECOND TIME AND GOT A PRETTY COLOR WE ALL LIKED.

PORTFOLIO ASSESSMENT AND EVALUATION

Assessment and evaluation of students by parents and teachers should include analyzing student work kept in portfolios. Portfolios have been used by artists and writers, in the past, to show the range and quality of work that a person is capable of doing. Students should be able to use this type of system to show where they are in the learning process, and what type of growth they are making. They will take pride in the work that is being included.

Portfolios are a wonderful tool for developing communication between teachers, parents, and students. They are also very helpful to the teacher to show concrete evidence of what further instruction might be needed.

Portfolios lead to student understanding of expectations teachers and parents have for them. They are especially helpful for getting children involved in assessing and evaluating their own work. It is very important for the student to be actively involved in the selection of work to be included as well as in the evaluation of that work. Students will understand more about themselves and where they need to improve as they reflect on the work they collect. They will increase their decision making skills as they analyze work and set goals for further growth. Portfolios truly help students to become self-directed learners.

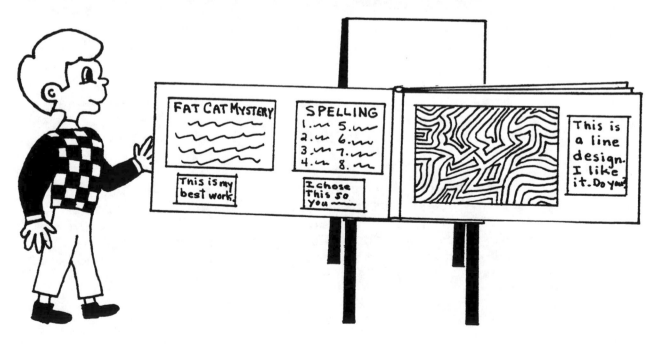

Following are possible considerations for setting up a portfolio system.

1. Obtain a scrapbook or make a scrapbook to use as a portfolio for each student. Let the student decorate the cover to personalize it, and find a place to store these scrapbooks in the classroom.

2. Set up a "Fat File", "Skinny File", Portfolio System as explained:

Fat Files

Fat files are boxes or containers where student work is placed as it is returned to the students after correction. Try setting up a system where you have a separate box for each group of five students, following alphabetical order.

It is also helpful if students are given consecutive numbers, according to alphabetical order, which they are to place at the top of each written assignment. Parents, aides, teachers, or students can easily sort out papers and place them into these boxes at any time, if both names and numbers are used by students.

At the end of a given time, every week or two, each group of five students will need to sit down together and sort out the work which has been placed in these boxes. Students will collect their own papers and place them in their skinny files.

Skinny Files

The skinny files are separate folders to be used by each student to save work that may be pasted into the portfolio scrapbooks. Legal size folders work well for this as they will be big enough to hold larger projects such as art work.

When students have collected a number of items in their skinny files, they will need to sort through them and decide which items they would like to include in their portfolios. This work will be saved in the skinny file until students have time to paste it into their portfolio scrapbooks. Papers and/or projects that a student does not intend to include in his/her portfolio should be taken home for parents to see at this time.

Portfolios

Portfolios are scrapbooks in which to paste work chosen from the skinny file. Each student will need to be given time to paste work into a portfolio and then write an assessment or fill out an evaluation form for work that is included.

Statements of students' goals for improvement can also be part of the portfolio evaluation. Teachers should write evaluative statements and positive comments next to work included in each student's portfolio.

Parents will read student and teacher evaluations and goal statements and write comments for their child. Comments may be about work that is well done, assignments that the child asked parents and teachers to notice, growth that can be seen, or they may be suggestions to help the child to set goals for further improvement. Students gain in self-esteem as they receive this positive feedback from teachers and parents.

Students can evaluate themselves on work in the portfolio by writing short notes about what they have done, or they may use preprinted evaluation forms. These forms can be filled out and pasted into the portfolio next to student work.

Sample forms are included on the following pages. They direct students to explain why they chose a certain piece or which learner characteristic they exhibited on an assignment. The following types of comments are found on the preprinted forms:

I chose this paper because..........

I chose this because I think I was generative when I..........

I selected this work so you could see how much I have improved in..........

I would like you to notice how organized I was when..........

I wanted you to see how industrious my group was when..........

I want you to see how collaborative my group was on this ....

Adapted from Robert Anthony's presentation on portfolio assessment at the Madrona Elementary School Nongraded Multi-Age Education Conference, Edmonds, WA, August, 1993. Some ideas he presented for evaluation forms were gathered from teachers in Sooke, British Columbia, Canada, and/or from the book Together is Better, written by Davies, Cameron, Politano, and Gregory. Peguis Publishers, Winnipeg, Canada.

PORTFOLIO EVALUATION FORMS

Name_____

The learner characteristic I exhibited
when I did this assignment was:

_____.

I chose this characteristic because:

_____

_____

_____

_____

_____

_____

Name_____

The learner characteristic I exhibited
when I did this assignment was:

_____.

I chose this characteristic because:

_____

_____

_____

_____

_____

_____

Name_____

The learner characteristic I exhibited
when I did this assignment was:

_____.

I chose this characteristic because:

_____

_____

_____

_____

_____

Name_____

The learner characteristic I exhibited
when I did this assignment was:

_____.

I chose this characteristic because:

_____

_____

_____

_____

_____

112   Adapted from Robert Anthony's presentation

PORTFOLIO EVALUATION FORMS

Name_____

I chose this paper because:

_____

_____

_____

_____

_____

Name_____

I chose this project because I am very proud of:

_____

_____

_____

_____

Name_____

This was my favorite piece of work because:

_____

_____

_____

_____

Name_____

I wanted you to see this award because:

_____

_____

_____

_____

Name_____

I selected this work so you could see how much I have improved in:

_____

_____

_____

_____

Name_____

I chose this so you could see how well I can:

_____

_____

_____

_____

Adapted from Robert Anthony's presentation

PORTFOLIO EVALUATION FORMS

Name_____

I chose this paper because I think I was:

_____

_____

_____

_____

Name_____

I would like you to notice how organized I was when:

_____

_____

_____

_____

Name_____

I wanted you to see how industrious my group was when:

_____

_____

_____

_____

Name_____

I chose this because I took a risk by trying:

_____

_____

_____

_____

Name_____

I want you to see how well my report followed this outline by:

_____

_____

_____

_____

Name_____

I wanted you to compare my first draft to my final draft because I improved in:

_____

_____

_____

_____

Adapted from Robert Anthony's presentation

PORTFOLIO EVALUATION FORMS

Name_____

I like this because I was thoughtful when:

_____

_____

_____

_____

Name_____

I want you to see how collaborative we were when we did this project, because:

_____

_____

_____

_____

Name_____

I chose this because I was very knowledgeable about:

_____

_____

_____

Name_____

I chose this because it was my very best:

_____

_____

_____

_____

Name_____

I selected this work so you could see how resourceful I was when:

_____

_____

_____

_____

Name_____

I chose this so you could see how confident I am that I can:

_____

_____

_____

115   Adapted from Robert Anthony's presentation

DAILY ASSIGNMENT RECORD

NAME_____   DATE_____

ASSIGNMENTS   **DATE DUE**

MONDAY	
TUESDAY	
WEDNESDAY	
THURSDAY	
FRIDAY	

INDEPENDENT WORK RECORD

How I Did in School this Week

Name_____

Date_____

Please think about how you did during independent work periods this week and write about your progress in each of the following areas:

Worked Independently
Worked Without Disturbing Others
Worked Cooperatively
Helped Others When Needed
Worked Neatly and Carefully
Finished My Work On Time

DAILY READING RECORD

NAME_____

DATE	BOOK	AUTHOR	PAGES

RECORD OF BOOKS I HAVE READ

NAME_____   DATE_____

Title	Author	Started	Finished

WEEKLY LEARNING CENTER PROGRESS REPORT

NAME_____   **WEEK OF**_____

WHAT I ACCOMPLISHED AT CENTERS THIS WEEK:

MONDAY	
TUESDAY	
WEDNESDAY	
THURSDAY	
FRIDAY	

HOW I FEEL ABOUT WHAT I ACCOMPLISHED THIS WEEK:

DAILY LEARNING CENTER PROGRESS REPORT

Name of Center_____   Date_____

Assignment_____

Time Spent at Center_____

What I Accomplished:

Goals for Next Time at This Center:

RESEARCH PROJECT REPORT

Name_____   Date_____

Topic of Report_____

Assignments	Date Due	Date Completed
Topic Chosen		
Information Located in Five Sources		
Notes Cards Labeled		
Notes Finished		
Rough Draft Written		
Rough Draft Revised and Edited		
Rough Draft Proofread		
Final Report Written		
Final Oral Presentation Written		
Final Oral Presentation Given		
Covers, Bibliography, Pictures Finished		
Final Report Turned In		

THEMATIC UNIT PROGRESS REPORT

Name_____ **Date**_____

Project_____ **Date Due**_____

What I've Finished:

What I Have Left to Do:

How Well I Feel I've Been Doing:

Goals for Improvement:

GROUP PROJECT EVALUATION

Name_____   **Date**_____

Partners_____

The topic we studied was:
The most important things we learned were:
The most interesting things we learned were:
The part of the project I did the best on was:
What our group could improve on next time is:
Next time I wish we could:

TEACHER MID-TERM PROGRESS REPORT

1=High Quality Performance   **2=Satisfactory Performance**
3=Need to Try Harder

Name_____   **Date**_____

_____Quality of Work Completed

_____Use of Class Time

_____Completing Work on Time

_____Behavior

_____Attitude

_____Working Independently

_____Working Cooperatively

_____Following Directions

_____Assuming Responsibility

GOALS FOR IMPROVEMENT:

Student Signature_____Teacher Signature_____

Parent Signature_____

STUDENT MID-TERM PROGRESS REPORT

Please rate _yourself_ on the following scale and _explain_ each rating:

1=High Quality Performance　　　　**2=Satisfactory Performance**
3=Need to Try Harder

Name_____　　　**Date**_____

_____Quality of Work Completed

_____Use of Class Time

_____Completing Work on Time

_____Behavior

_____Attitude

_____Working Independently

_____Working Cooperatively

_____Following Directions

_____Assuming Responsibility

GOALS FOR IMPROVEMENT:

Student Signature_____Teacher Signature_____

Parent Signature_____

126

A GLOSSARY OF TERMS FOR MULTI-AGE INSTRUCTION

Aesthetic Growth
Growth in enthusiasm and appreciation of the arts, in exploring, expressing, visualizing, interpreting and creating art forms, etc.

Arbitrary Standard
Absolute goal or expectation to be met by all students, regardless of individual differences.

Child-Focused Classroom
A classroom where instruction is focused on the needs of individual children, where children have choices and must take a part of the responsibility for their own learning.

Continuous Progress
The uninterrupted advancement of pupils in all significant areas of development; moving forward in learning as rapidly and as smoothly as possible.

Continuum of Learning
A sequenced set of learning objectives, which all students need to learn as they progress.

Cooperative Learning
Working together and helping each other to find answers, solve problems, seek solutions, and gain knowledge.

Critical Thinking
Reasonable, reflective thinking that is focused on what to believe or do, while being objective and logical.

Decision-Making
Selecting from among alternatives.

Emotional Growth
Growth in the areas of developing positive self-concepts, expressing emotions in socially acceptable ways, developing independence, accepting challenges, feeling pride in accomplishments, enjoying living, coping with change, etc.

Flexible Grouping
A variation of all types of grouping, with change as needed.

127

Flexible Scheduling

Scheduling that changes according to the needs of the students and time needed for thematic instruction, rather than following isolated periods of time for separate subjects.

Heterogeneous Grouping

The practice of grouping students together who represent wide ranges of ability.

Higher-Level Thinking Skills

Skills involving more than recall of information, such as analyzing, applying, evaluating and putting ideas together in novel ways.

Homogeneous Grouping

The practice of grouping students for the purpose of forming instructional groups that have similarities in regard to certain factors that affect learning.

Indicators

Outcomes to be verified, proving that an objective has been met.

Inquiry Approach

Learning through predicting, seeking solutions, or solving problems as a basis for instruction.

Instructional Strategies

The way children are taught, including the activities they use, and the role of the classroom teacher.

Integrated Curriculum

Curriculum with connections between the subjects; active linkages between fields of knowledge; different subjects brought together into one area of study, using the interdisciplinary approach to learning.

Intellectual Growth

Growth in the area of sustaining curiosity, developing the skills and attitudes necessary for independent learning, developing thinking processes, using language to facilitate learning, developing ways to communicate effectively, etc.

Interest Grouping

Grouping according to the topics of interest to students.

Keyboarding

The process of learning to use the typewriter and computer keyboards.

Learning Centers

Areas of the classroom containing a variety of small-group and individualized materials, with self-directed activities for regular instructional needs or enrichment.

Learning Styles

Methods of perceiving information: visual, auditory, tactile, or kinesthetic.

Lifelong Learners

Students who will be able to think for themselves, make wise decisions, be responsible and dependable, self-directed, and able to do research and manage their time effectively.

Literature-Based Program

Reading program using childrens' literature, with novels as the primary resource for instruction.

Multi-Age Grouping

Grouping with widely varying ages, abilities, interests, backgrounds and experiences.

Narrative Reporting

Reporting in paragraph form about the child's total school experiences, behavior patterns, development in various areas, attitudes, interests, strengths, problem areas, goals, etc.

Peer Evaluation

Students helping each other to improve performance by making judgments, correcting errors through editing activities, and helping each other to understand corrections.

Peer Tutoring

Teaching by individuals of one's own age group, ability group, interest group, or grade level.

Physical Growth

Growth in development of motor skills, fitness, nutrition and care of the body, and personal safety.

Portfolio

A folder or scrapbook containing work samples, performance data, observations, writing samples, tests, etc., used as a basis for student evaluation and assessment.

Problem Solving

Analyzing and finding the answer to a perplexing or difficult situation.

Process

The ability of the student to make a connection or to see patterns so that the transfer of information from one situation to another occurs.

Process Skills

To identify, select, analyze, and communicate.

Random Grouping

Grouping without any special method of organization, without paying attention to the abilities, interests, needs, etc.

Self-Directed Activities

Activities that are individualized, where children may choose from alternatives, and work independently without teacher direction.

Self-Directed Students

Students who are dependable, responsible, able to think for themselves, and make wise choices and decisions.

Self-Pacing Materials

Materials that are individualized and self-correcting so that students work alone at their own rates, correcting themselves as they go and keeping track of their own performances and progress.

Social Growth

Growth in the areas of sharing, cooperating, respecting others, developing friendships, appreciating cultural identity, valuing and respecting individual differences, etc.

Student-Centered Curriculum

Curriculum presented by the teacher to fit the needs and choices of individuals, where students are partly responsible for determining the scope and sequence of activities, and for their own learning.

Student-Focused Classroom

A classroom environment where the teacher assumes the role of facilitator of learning; offering choices, materials and resources, guiding scope and sequence, and sharing responsibility for learning with students.

Teacher-Centered Curriculum

Curriculum planned by the teacher for all students to cover at the same time with little choice for students, and without regard to the variety of individual levels and interests.

Teacher Facilitator

Teacher in the role of learning guide, offering choices, helping students find materials and determining scope and sequence for the student to follow.

Teacher-Focused Classroom

Teacher as information provider and learning director.

Team Teaching

Two or more teachers working and planning together, using the strengths and interests of each to improve instruction, by planning an overall and coordinated program for their students.

Thematic Teaching

Teaching with units, following themes, encompassing all subject areas, and stressing interrelationships between subjects.

Whole Language

A method of teaching all communication skills (reading, writing, spelling, speaking, listening) together using a literature base and a wealth of materials to integrate language processes into a meaningful whole.

Words and Definitions are taken from The Edmonds Project: A School of Choice for the 21st Century, a State Grant Submitted for the 21st Century, by the Staff of Madrona Nongraded School. Co-authored by Janet Caudill Banks.

REFERENCES, RESOURCES, AND CREDITS

Adler, Mortimer J. *Reforming Education: The Opening of the American Mind.* New York, NY: Macmillan Publishing Company, 1988.

Anderson, Barry F. *The Complete Thinker: A Handbook of Techniques for Creative and Critical Problem Solving.* Englewood Cliffs, NJ: Prentice-Hall, 1980.

Anderson, Carolyn. *The Brain Stretchers. (Book 2).* Troy, MI: Midwest Publications.

Anderson, Robert H., and Barbara Nelson Pavan. *Nongradedness: Helping It to Happen.* Lancaster, PA: Technomic Publishing Co., Inc., 1993.

Anthony, Robert J., Terry D. Johnson, Norma I. Mickelson, and Alison Preece. *Evaluating Literacy, A Perspective for Change.* University of Victoria, British Columbia. Portsmouth, NH: Heinemann Publishing Co., 1991.

--------. *Refocusing Evaluation.* University of Victoria, British Columbia. Portsmouth, NH: Heinemann Publishing Co.

Banks, Janet Caudill. *Creative Projects for Independent Learners.* Edmonds, WA: CATS Publications, 1995.

--------. *Developing Research Skills.* Edmonds, WA: CATS Publications, 1995.

--------. *Enhancing Research Skills.* Edmonds, WA: CATS Publications, 1995.

--------. *Essential Learnings of Mathematics.* Edmonds, WA: CATS Publications, 1996.

Barbe, Walter B., and Raymond Swassing with Michael N. Malone. *Teaching Through Modality Strengths: Concepts and Practices.* Columbus, OH: Zaner-Bloser, Inc., 1979.

Bellanca, James, and Robin Fogarty. *Blueprints for Thinking in the Cooperative Classroom.* Palatine, IL: Skylight Publishing, 1991.

132

Bloom, Benjamin S. *All Our Children Learning*. New York, NY: McGraw Hill, 1982.

--------. *Developing Talent in Young People*. New York, NY: Ballantine Books, 1985.

--------. *Human Characteristics and School Learning*. New York, NY: McGraw Hill, 1976.

--------. *Taxonomy of Educational Objectives: Cognitive Domain*. New York, NY: David McKay, 1956.

Bredekamp, Sue, ed. *Developmentally Appropriate Practice in Early Childhood Programs Serving Children From Birth Through Age 8*. Washington, DC: National Association for the Education of Young Children, 1987.

Bruner, Jerome. *Toward a Theory of Instruction*. Cambridge, MA: Belknap Press, 1975.

Canfield, Jack, and Harold C. Wells. *100 ways to enhance self-concept in the classroom: a handbook for teachers and parents*. Englewood Cliffs, NJ: Prentice-Hall, Inc., 1976.

Carbo, Marie. "Reading Styles Change Between Second and Eighth Grade." *Educational Leadership* 40 (February 1983): 56-59.

Chase, Larry. *The Other Side of the Report Card: A How-to-do-it Program for Affective Education*. Glenville, IL: Scott, Foresman and Co., 1975.

Costa, Arthur L. *Developing Minds: A Resource Book for Teaching Thinking*. Alexandria, VA: Association for Supervision and Curriculum Development, 1985.

Davies, Anne, Caren Cameron, Colleen Politano, and Kathleen Gregory. *Together is Better: Collaborative Assessment, Evaluation, & Reporting*. Winnipeg, Canada: Peguis Publishers.

de Bono, Edward. *The Five Day Course in Thinking*. New York, NY: Basic Books, 1967.

Dunn, Rita, and Angela Bruno. *Teaching Students Through Their Individual Learning Styles: A Practical Approach*. Reston, VA: Reston Publishing Company, Inc.,1978.

Ellis, Susan S., and Susan F. Whalen. *Cooperative Learning: Getting Started*. New York, NY: Scholastic, 1990.

Edmonds School District Nongraded Staff. *The Edmonds Project: A School of Choice for the 21st Century*. Edmonds, WA: Edmonds School District, 1989.

Fern, Leif. *Teaching for Thinking: 311 Ways to Cause Creative Behavior*. San Diego, CA: Kabyn Books.

Frank, Marjorie. *If You're Trying to Teach Kids How to Write, You've Gotta Have This Book!* Nashville, TN: Incentive Publications, Inc., 1979.

Gamberg, Ruth, Winniefred Kwak, Meredith Hutchings, and Judy Altheim. *Learning and Loving It: Theme Studies in the Classroom*. Portsmouth, NH: Heinemann Publishing Co., 1988.

Gilbert, Judith. *Interdisciplinary Learning: A Resource Guide*. Colorado Department of Education, May, 1987.

Gardner, Howard. *Frames of Mind*. New York, NY: Basic Books, 1983.

George, Paul. *How to Untrack Your School*. Alexandria VA: Association for Supervision and Curriculum Development, 1992.

Glasser, William, M.D. *Control Theory in the Classroom*. New York, NY: Harper Perennial, 1986.

--------.*Schools Without Failure*. New York, NY: Harper and Row, 1969.

--------.*The Quality School: Managing Students Without Coercion*. New York, NY: Harper Perennial, 1992.

Goodlad, John I. *A Place Called School*. New York, NY: McGraw Hill, 1984.

--------.and Robert H. Anderson. *The Nongraded Elementary School*. New York, NY: Teachers College Press, 1987.

Grant, Jim. *Developmental Education in the 1990's*. Rosemont, NJ: Modern Learning Press, 1989.

--------.and Bob Johnson. *A Common Sense Guide to Multiage Practices*. Columbus, OH: Teacher's Publishing Group, 1994.

Gregorc, Anthony F. *An Adult's Guide to Style*. Maynard, MA: Gabriel Systems, 1982.

Harrison, Allen, and Robert M. Bramson. *Styles of Thinking: Strategies for Asking Questions, Making Decisions, and Solving Problems.* Garden City, NY: Anchor Press, Doubleday, 1982.

Hart, Leslie. *How the Brain Works*. New York, NY: Basic Books, Inc., 1975.

Hunter, Madeline. *How to Change to a Nongraded School*. Alexandria, VA: Association for Supervision and Curriculum Development, 1992.

Jacobs, Heidi. *Interdisciplinary Curriculum: Design and Implementation*. Alexandria, VA: Association for Supervision and Curriculum Development, 1989.

Johnson, David W., and Roger T. Johnson. *Learning Together and Alone: Cooperative, Competitive, and Individualistic Learning*. Needham Heights, MA: Allyn and Bacon, 1991.

--------.Edythe Holubec and Pat Roy. *Circles of Learning: Cooperation in the Classroom*. Edina, MA: Interaction.

Kovalik, Susan. *Brain Compatible Learning and Integrated, Thematic Instruction*. San Jose, CA: Summer Institute, 1989.

Krathwohl, David. *Taxonomy of Educational Objectives: Handbook II, Affective Domain*. West Nyack, NY: David McKay Publishing Company, 1964.

Leonard, George B. *Education and Ecstasy*. New York, NY: Dell Publishing Company, Inc., 1968.

Miller, Bruce A. *The Multigrade Classroom: A Resource Handbook for the Small Rural Schools*. Portland, OR: Northwest Regional Education Laboratory, 1989.

--------.*Training Guide for the Multigrade Classroom: A Resource Handbook for Small, Rural Schools*. Portland, OR: Northwest Regional Educational Laboratory, 1990.

Oklahoma State Department of Education. *One of a Kind: A Practical Guide to Learning Styles*. State Board of Education, 1983.

Paul, Richard, A.J.A. Binker, D. Jensen, and H. Kreklau. *Critical Thinking Handbook 4th-6th Grades*. Rohnert Park, CA: Center for Critical Thinking and Moral Critique, 1987.

Polette, Nancy. *Pick a Pattern for Creative Writing*. O'Fallon, MO: Book Lures, Inc., 1979.

Province of British Columbia. *Primary Program Foundation Document*. Victoria, B.C.: Crown Publications, 1990.

Rathbone, Charles, Anne Bingham, Peggy Dorta, and Molly McClaskey. *Multiage Portraits: Teaching and Learning in Mixed-age Classrooms*. Peterborough, NH: Crystal Springs Books, 1993.

Routman, Regie. *Transitions: From Literature to Literacy*. Portsmouth, NH: Heinemann Publishing Co., 1988.

Slavin, Robert. *Cooperative Learning*. New York, NY: Longman Press, 1983.

SDE Sourcebook. *Multiage Classrooms: The Ungrading of America's Schools*. Peterborough, NH: Society for Developmental Education, 1993.

--------.*Staying Focused on the Children: Creating Child-Centered Classrooms Where All Children Learn, All Children Succeed*. Peterborough, NH: Society for Developmental Education, 1994.

Taylor, Dr. Roger. *Using Integrated, Thematic Teaching Strategies to Increase Student Achievement and Motivation: Resource Handbook*. Bellevue, WA: Bureau of Education and Research, 1989.

Thornburg, Pamela, and David Thornburg. *The Thinker's Toolbox: A Practical and Easy Approach to Creative Thinking*. Palo Alto, CA: Dale Seymour Publications, 1989.

Williams, Linda Verlee. *Teaching for the Two-Sided Mind*. New York, NY: Simon and Schuster, 1986.

Wolf, d.P. "What's in It?: Examining Portfolio Assessment." *Educational Leadership*, April, 1989.